GLOBALISATION OF ECONOMY
Vision for the Future

GLOBALISATION OF ECONOMY

Vision for the Future

Edited by
B. MOHANAN

GYAN

Published by

Gyan Publishing House
5, Ansari Road
Daryaganj, New Delhi-110002
Phone: 011-47034999, 9811692060
E-mail: books@gyanbooks.com

Distribution Network
gyanbooks.com
India, USA, Canada, UK, Australia, France

ISBN: 978-93-6280-569-0 (PB)

First Published, 2024

Printed at: Gyan Press, Delhi.

Globalisation of Economy: Vision For the Future
Author: B. Mohanan

EDITOR'S NOTE

One of the far reaching consequences of the disintegration of Soviet Union and the resultant decline of the socialist system seems to be a tendency toward a gradual erosion of sovereignty of states everwhere, particularly in the southern hemisphere. The modern state, as it exists today, is under erosion. The very legitimacy of the state is being questioned. It is argued by scholars that the challenges to the known pattern of state structure come from two diametrically opposite sources. One is from the international societal network, the vehicle of corporate captialism. The other is from within the hitherto marginalised groups, organised on the lines of primordial identities, demand for freedom, autonomy and distributive justice. A third factor that bears potentialities to subvert the fragile state structures of the third world regions could be the developmental assistance to these countries from the industrialised west pumped through non-governmental organisations. Consequently the established structures of governance are being eroded gradually.

What is going to be the future of nation state? Will there emerge a supranational organisation in the place of the present nation state? Or will the states get fragmented and give birth to mini-and micro-states to satisfy the urge of assertive ethnonationalism for equity and justice? Or, will some pan-national formation grow out of a possible convergence of ethnicity and class? What are the threat perceptions of the various states? How are they planning to overcome these threats to their political, economic and environmental security? What exactly is the nature of challenges faced by the states on account of environmental degradation? What impact will it have on the economic development of these states? These and related questions have to be answered squarely before one thinks of the future of the nation-states.

Barry Buzan, a well known analyst in the field of international relations, has written recently that the historians of tomorrow will mark 1989 as the end of the twentieth century. He says that the period upto 1989 can be treated as a self-contained unit in which wars unleashed ideological rivalries and ideological rivalries unleashed wars, both "hot" and "cold". Fascism and communism developed as a challenge to liberalism. Both capitalism and communism joined hands to eliminate fascism. But in the post-second world war period capitalism was pitted against communism especially during the period of cold war which ended peacefully in 1989. This resulted in the collapse of communism and strengthening the forces of capitalism. The over enthusiastic votaries of corporate capitalism celebrated the event with great excitement and came out with the much publicised "end of history" thesis. Fukuyama, the author of this thesis, later talked about the post-historical society. What Fukuyama projected cannot be dismissed casually. Global dominance by the West over the economy, polity, society and culture of the rest of the world, is surely, the underlying thrust of the so called post-historical society. Such an international society is in the making. Institutions and regimes that developed during the cold war era are pressed into service to construct it. The law of the sea regime, the nuclear non-proliferation regime, the IMF, World Bank, the OECD, the GATT/WTO and the G-7 are the main pillars of the new international societal network. It is quite logical that now there is hardly any talk about national self-reliance anywhere in the South as these countries have been forced to abandon the dearly nursed concept of New International Economic Order (NIEO) based on the principles of equity, fairplay and justice in international political and economic relations.

The transnational corporations, transnational banks, UN Security Council and Multilateral Financial institutions will come to be controlled and directed by the G-7 nations. The trade, commercial and security interests of these nations will be protected through their bipolar structure of the world has been changed to a unipolar (or depolarised)? one. The nations not conforming with the G-7 led by US mainly, will be isolated. Potential threats like Libya and Iraq have already been attacked. Cuba and like minded nations still have sanctions imposed on them. Though inter-state warfare may be done away with, intra-state conflicts may arise which may be extremely bloody in nature with the use of sophisticated arms. The reason for this can be rising ethnic natinalism and socio-economic inequality among the people of a nation itself. The main victims of these new conflicts maight be nation-states of Eurasia and the third world. The US is also likely to mould the former Soviet Republics in its own image as was the case of Japan and Germany after the Second World War. The conditions in the third world will be worse off that it is today. Inequality, deprivation and unrest will be widespread in them. Important issues like eco-portection, environment protection and peace will be given priority according to the views of the G-7 nations.

"Greed is good" seems to be the ebullient message of the commercial consumer culture that is reared carefully by the international societal network. This greed has been amply demonstrated in the manner in which the Americans and other G-7 members fought inch by inch to get their view point accepted by poor southern countries in the Urugay Round of the GATT. The US negotiators could get away with what they wanted, when the Dunkel Draft was finally endorsed by the representatives of 117 countries of the world at the Urugay Round at Geneva on 15th December 1993. That day witnessed the unconditional surrender of third world countries out of sheer helplessness. This kind of a total surrender of the countries in the South is, infact, a direct consequence of the countries in the South is, infact, a direct consequence of the collapse of Soviet Union as also the disunity among the third world countries-a natural finale to the Globalisation-Liberalization syndrome.

The new World Trade Organisation (WTO) which replaced the GATT came into existence, on 1 January 1995, as the third pillar of the international economic regime. In addition to commodity trade, it will deal with services across the borders like insurance and tourism. It will protect intellectual property like patents, copyrights and brands. It also covers aagriculture and textiles. The goal of this organisation is to oversee global trade. It is armed with a standing dispute resolution body and the muscle to impose severe sanctions against those who violate its rules. The move is to have a centralised control over global commerce. WTO represents multilateralism of the highest order. It is worth noting here that India, in order to meet its obligations under the WTO, amended the patent Act 1970 and customs Tariff Act 1975 through a late night promulgation of two ordinances on 31 December 1994, one day before WTO was born.

At the same time, it is also well known that the new rules on ending trade disputes and related matters are not going to be strictly followed by the industrialised West, particularly the United States. It is a universal truth all are equal before law but some are more equal than others. This is evident from the dispute between United States and Japan over the sales of cars and automobile parts. The accord reached between the United States and Japan over this issue stands testimony to the triumph of bilateralism at the doorsteps of high-pitch multilateralism. The US decision to pullout of the talks on financial services is another instance to show that the US will not adhere to WTO rules and multilateralism. Eventhough United States if America is currnetly the high priest of multilateralism, that country will pressurise and terrorise other countries with bilateralism and unilateralism if the situation so warrants.

As the twenty first century unfolds with the West in commanding position, it will definitely be an era of economic and cultural recolonisation for the rest of the world. The legitimacy of the local customs and identities have been corroded considerably. The hollow consumer culture of the West has been penetrating deeply into the weaker societies and this in turn introduces styles, ideas and aspirations alien to these societies. This has created the impression that anything Western is good and everything non. Western is bad.

The ecological component adds yet another dimension to the problem. The current political economy of the "North" is built upon massive use of energy and resources. In fact the last Gulf War was to ensure uninterrupted supply of cheap oil for the maintenance of the capitalist way of life.

The resource intensive model of "developement" leads to large scale environmental crisis—Green house effect, changing climatic patterns, rising sea levels, ozone depletion, toxic waste, deforestation, rapid global depletion of species diversity, localised dangers of soil erosion, acid precipitation, pollution, toxic contamination, etc.

II

As is the case with any other third world country, we have also been forced to launch the globalisation, liberalisation and marketisation programmes as prescribed by the Bank-Fund G-7 combine. Consequently we are now undergoing a reverse historical process. The first half of the century was the period of decolonisation and the latter half the era of re-colonisation. The basic principles of governance as enshrined in the Preamble of Constitution of the country are being undermined. The words 'sovereign' and 'socialist' given in the preamble have now become more beautiful exopressions. The demos, represented by the Indian Parliament, have not been taken into confidence while vital policy decisions of long lasting import are taken by the executive and bureaucratic leadership.

The visionary ideals of our great leaders like Gandhi and Nehru have been done away with quietly. We celebrate their anniversaries just to be sure that they remain buried. Their principles are not to be practised. Godse killed Gandhi physically. We are killing the ideological Gandhi everyday. In Gandhi's vision mass production was to mean production by the masses, denoting people's participation. Machinery was to exist for man and not the otherway round as at present.

The new economic policy has been proving futile as the foreign consumer goods are beyond the reach of 80% of the population. The trickle-down argument is meaningless in the Indian context. Nehru might be weeping in his grave seeing the sad state of affairs. In the initial years of Independence he took the strong stand that we should not degrade ourselves to the level of international mendicants. He called upon Indians to achieve dignity through hard work.

The vicious circle of dept and more debt to pay the former ones will end in a debt trap. It is a foregone conclusion that debts will make us accept conditionalities of the lenders.

This is generally the academic perception of our problems. Most of the politicians and bureaucrats do not subscribe to the above view. A consensus has already emerged as major political parties from the extreme right to the mainstream left say that the reform process should stay. It seems that the ruling elite came to the conclusion that replacing state with the market would eradicate poverty and solve problems of unemployment, underemployment, population explosion etc which evaded solution for more than four decades.

III

Raising the four Es-Economic Globalisation, Environment, Ecology and Ethnicity, the Institute for the Study of Developing Areas organised a three day national seminar in March with the finacial support of Indian Council of Social Science Research-Southern Regional Centre, Hyderabad and the Department of Science, Technology and Environment, Government of Kerala. The Seminar was spread over four sessions under the rubrics 'Globalisation of the Economy and the Emerging International Order', 'Issues on Sustainable Agricultural Development', 'Ecology and Environment' and 'Ethnicity, Neo nationalism and the Emerging from the fields of natural science, Social Sciences, Politics and NGOs. However, only selected papers that dealt with the socio-political consequences of economic globalisation are included in the present volume.

The papers were generally of three categories—realistic, pessimistic and optimistic. Prof. Ramachandran Nair has contributed two papers to the volume. In the first paper on World Economic Order, he indentifies the emerging trends in global economic realities. He argues that the spirit of multilaterism is threatened by growing regioinalism as evidenced by the European Union, the North American Free Trade Association (NAFTA) etc. More than that the USA still continues its single track, multitrack and fast track approaches to global economic relations. The USA wants to protect it hegemony and retain its super power status by keeping the emerging global economic order as unjust and inequitous as it was since the second world war. In his second paper he takes a critical view of the Union budget 95-96. He argues that even after the presentation of four budgets by the reform architect Dr. Manmohan Singh, the basic weaknesses of the Indian Economy have not changed a bit.

Prof. Tom Travis discusses the main features of the Emerging International System and suggests that United States will be advantaged in the emerging world order. Prof. Ninan Koshy cites the major developments which has distorted the vision for the future. The first was the declaration of the new world order by President Bush just before the announcement of the Persian Gulf War. The second development was the breakdown of the Soviet block as a whole. This has caused an imbalance in the power structure with America occupying the sole super power structure.

Dr.N.A. Karim talks about information imperialism. The world is totally dependent on the western media for information especially at the time of crisis like the Gulf war. The four big international news agencies that control and regulate international newsflow are western and they all work with a clear commitment to uphold and safeguard the western political, economic and military-strategic interests. Dr. Nanda Mohan and Dr.P.N. Sankaran try to highlight the role, prospects and problems of the cooperatives in the 21st century against the background of the process of globalisation and market lliberalisation with special reference to India. They argue that the social and economic cost of failure of the cooperatives in the new dispensation would be very high, given the extent of rural poverty and unemployment prevelent in India. Sri. Niyathi looks into the implications of the present liberalisation policy in export performance. Dr.G.K. Rajendran makes an evaluation of the industrial policy 1991 and tells us that the new policy would speed up industrialisation. Shri. J. Prabhash analyses the impact of the New Economic Policy on different social classes and concludes that for the poor, the emerging order spells economic, political and social marginalisation. Dr. Gopal Singh, Shri Rajinder Kaur and Prem R Bharadwaj and N.S. Gehlot assess the emerging trend in Indian politics in the context of the disintegration of Soviet Union and decline of socialism as a model of economic development. Dr. K.M. Menon argues that Tourism has an important economic role to play. Tourism is different from other industries. In the new situation the marketing of Tourism has changed from the concept of profit making to consumer satisfaction. Dr. R.K. Suresh Kumar in his thought provoking paper argues that under globalisation regime the role of Parliament stands diminished. Important policy decisions are taken by bureaucracy. In the globalisation process the parliament, the representative body of Indian people has been relegated to the position of a mute victim.

I deem it a privilege to present these worthwhile papers to a wider audience.

Dr. B. Mohanan
Director (Hon)

Institute for the Study of
Devloping Area (ISDA)
Thiruvananthapuram

Contents

1

New Economic Reforms in India—Liberalising a Command Economy—An Evaluation of New Industrial Policy—1991

Dr. G.K. Rajendran

Introduction

From mid-1991 the Indian economy is in the process of implementing a structural adjustment programme. The New Economic Policy that was introduced since July 1991 included interest rate liberalisation, encouragement of Private Industry, abolition of export subsidies, elimination of import licensing, devaluation, new trade policy, new Industrial Policy and many other economic reforms. There is a common thread running through all these measures. The new policy sought to achieve an improvement in the functioning of the various entities whether they be in the private or public sector by injecting an element of competition. The Industrial Policy seeks to bring about a greater competitive domestic environment. This paper analyses some elements in the new Industrial Policy—1991 followed by a package included in the structural adjustment programmes.

The Industrial development of a country largely depends on the Industrial Policy adopted by the Government. The first Industrial Policy resolution of Independent India was announced an April 6, 1948. The new Industrial Policy as part of the structural adjustment programme was announced on 24 July, 1991.

Objectives

1. Speedy Industrialisation.
2. Correct the weakness of the Industrial Sector.
3. Sustained growth in productivity and employment.
4. Attain International competitiveness.
5. Preservation of environment and efficient use of the available resources.

In order ot attain these objectives the following changes were introduced in the new Industrial Policy.

SALIENT FEATURES OF THE NEW POLICY

1. Reduced Role for the Public Sector

The areas reserved for the Public Sector have been reduced from 17 to 8. These are:

Arms and ammunition,

atomic energy,

coal and lignite,

mineral oils,

mining of iron ore, manganese ore, gold and diamond,

mining of copper, lead, zinc, tin,

wolfram minerals specified in the Schedule to Atomic Energy Order 1953,

and railway transport.

II. Disinvestment of Govt. Equity in Public Sector Undertakings

In order to introduce professionalism in management and to raise revenue to reduce the fiscal deficit, the new policy aims at a gradual disinvestment of govt. equity upto 49% over a period of time. With 51% equity the PSU will continue to be under govt. control.

III. Delicensing

Except 18 industries which will continue to be under licensing due to 'Strategic, Social, Environmental and Safety reasons' all other industries have been delicensed. The important industries which require compulsory licensing include coal and lignite, petroleum products, alcoholic drinks, sugar, animal fats, cigars, asbestos and asbestos-based products, plywood and wood-based products, raw hides and skins and leather, motor cars, paper and newsprint except bagasse-based units, electronic, aerospace and defence equipment, industrial explosives, hazardous chemicals, drugs and pharmaceuticals, entertainment electronics and white goods.

IV. Changes in the MRTP Act

The practice of defining monopolies on the basis of assets and dominant undertakings on the basis of market share has been given up. The threshold limit of Rs.100 crores in assets, which made a company a monopoly, has been removed. Big industrial houses (formarly defined as monopoly houses on the basis of assets) do not need prior govt. approval for expansion, setting up of new units, amalgamations, mergers, etc.

The new policy lays emphasis on the regulation and control of monopolistic, restrictive and unfair trade practices. Public Sector undertakings will also be included under the MRTP Act.

V. Changes in FERA

The Foreign Exchange Regulation Act has been amended and far-reaching reforms introduced. The salient features are:

1. 51% foreign equity participation in 34 select industries.
2. 100% foreign equity participation by NRIs and Overseas Corporate Bodies (OCBs) in high priority areas like 100% EOUs, power generation, etc.
3. Automatic approval for the import of capital goods provided the imports are financed by foreign equity or if the cost of import of capital goods does not exceed 25% of investment upto a maximum of Rs. 2 crores (This condition has been subsequently withdrawn).
4. Restrictions on the use of brand names/trademarks, etc. have been removed.

VI. Reforms in the Capital Market

The capital market has been freed from govt. control. The office of the Controller of Capital Issues has been abolished. The watchdog body SEBI has been given statutory powers.

Recent Changes

The reforms were continued in 1992 and 1993. The latest round of reforms includes the following :

1. Private investment in exploration and refining has been allowed in the hydro carbon sector.
2. Motor cars, consumer electronics and white goods have been delicensed.
3. Foreign Institutional investment has been allowed in the capital market.
4. Existing foreign subsidiaries have been allowed to raise their equity to 51% at a price approved by the AGM.
5. Indian companies have been allowed to raise capital abroad.

Assesment

The new policy aims at liberalising the economy and integrating it with the global economy. It is a response to the problems of industrialisation internally and the emerging International scenario externally. An objective analysis of our industrial performance since independence will reveal the fact that our industrial policy based on the 'commanding heights principle' and 'leadership role for the State' did succeed in giving us a strong industrial infrastructure, a vibrant and modern industrial sector and a resilient economy. At a time when the private sector was facing resource constraints, our policy gave us a modern infrastructure which can now act as the runway from which the economy can take off towards sustained growth.

But this achievement should not prevent us from accepting the fact that the very same policy created what Rajaji called 'The licence-permit-quota raj'. It created a highly inefficient public sector which has almost become a millstone around the economy's neck. It led to a massive bureaucracy which perfected the art of stifling initiative and killing enterprise. Many provisions in the policies, though with good intentions, created distortions within the economy and contrained growth and industrialisation. The public sector with an investment of over Rs. 3,00,000 crores in 1,150 industrial undertakings (900 units in states and 250 in the Central Sector) yields negative returns. Even though the Central Undertakings are better managed, their performance is far from satisfactory. Data on 206 public undertakings provided by the Bureau of Public Enterprises for 1989-90 are self revealing. This data reveal that the total funds employed in the 206 Central Undertakings were Rs. 1, 50, 317. 4 crores. The net profit on this massive investment was only Rs. 2,946 crores. Out of this 2,946 crores, Rs. 2,392 crores were accounted by the oil monopolies. Apart from the oil sector profits came from govt. monopolies like Hindustan Copper. Hindustan Zinc, Hindustan Tin, Hindustan Lead, etc. If the profits of these monopolies are excluded the returns on this massive funds employed are negative. In those areas where the public sector was competing with the private sector like Cycles, Scooters, Cement, Tyre, Drugs, etc. the public sector had accumulated losses several times their equity capital.

The following table reveals the performance in growth rate of Selected Industries

Average Annual Growth Rates of Industrial Production.
Sectoral Growth Rates (Percentages)

Period	*Mining*	*Manufacturing*	*Electricity*	*Total*
1955-56 to 1965-66	7.1	6.2	12.9	3.2
1965-66 to 1975-76	3.0	3.3	7.8	3.9
1975-76 to 1980-81	3.3	4.5	7.6	3.4
1981-82 to 1984-85	12.7	5.8	8.9	7.0
1985-86 to 1989-90	5.7	8.8	9.4	8.5
1990-91	3.5	9.2	8.6	8.4

Source: Government of India, Central Statistical Organisation.

Judicious privatisation is the only sensible way out of this problem. The policy of disinvestment of govt. equity can be used to professionalise the management of these PSUs.

The Finance Minister, Dr. Manmohan Singh, has managed to turn the Indian Economy around in less than five years, from the brink of bankruptcy to the threshold of high growth path. The reforms has helped Indian business to go beyond the traditional frontiers of protected domestic markets. Liberalisation of trade and investment besides Industrial delicensing have already brought about big changes in the economy.

The remarkable progress has been made by Indian Economy since the difficult days of the 1991 economic crisis with an overall growth rate of 0.9 per cent in 1991-92 to an expected growth rate of 5.3 per cent in 1994-95. The new Industrial Policy as part of the new economic reforms shows remarkable progress in the Industrial growth. The following table explains the percentage growth of Industrial Production in India.

Annual Growth rates of Major Sectors of Industry (Percent)

Year	*Mining*	*Manufacturing*	*Electricity*	*General*
1990-91	4.5	8.9	7.8	8.3
1991-92	0.6	−0.8	8.5	0.6
1992-93	0.6	2.2	5.0	2.3
1993-94	2.5	3.6	7.4	4.1
1994-95	6.2	8.3	7.7	8.0

Source: **Economic Survey Government of india 1994.**

The overall Industrial Production during 1994, 95 registered an increase of 8.0 per cent in manufacturing supported by a growth of 8.3 per cent in manufacturing, 7.7 per cent in electricity and 6.2 per cent in mining.

When we closely examine the Industrial Production before and after the introduction of the new Policy, it is evident that the reforms were capable of fixing the edifice of the economy which started shaking during 1991-92. After a decade of uninterrupted and impressive growth, Industrial Production stagnated during the fiscal year ended March 1992. We observe the quarterly growth rates in Industrial Production preceding and succeeding the new Policy clearly exhibit the miraculous changes that have taken place in the economy. The last quarter of 1991-92 and the first quarter of 1992-93 showed signs of a modest industrial recovery as they registered growth rate of 1.6 per cent and 3.5 per cent respectively. The following figures show the percentage variation of industrial production before and after 1990-91.

During 1990-91 the growth rate was 8.3 per cent, it declined steeply to 0.6 per cent in 1991-92. Thereafter it gradually began to regain from the stagnation of 1991-92 to 2.3 per cent in 1992-93 and 4.1 per cent in 1994-95.

A 1.5 per cent decline in the manufacturing sector in 1991-92 was the singlemost important reason for the decline in industrial activity in the year.

The following table illustrates the performance of Indian industry over several years keeping the index of Industrial Production as 100 in 1980-81.

Item	*1990-91*	*'91-92*	*'92-93*	*'93-94*	*'94-95*	*Annual growth rate %*	*% change over previous year*				
						'81-91	*90-91*	*91-92*	*92-93*	*93-94*	*94-95*
1. Index of Industrial Production	212.5	212.5	215.6	225.4	273.3	7.8	8.2	0.00	1.5	4.5	5.2
(a) Manufacturing	207.8	204.5	205.7	214.9	226.4	7.6	9.0	—1.6	0.6	4.5	5.1
(b) Mining and quarrying	221.2	211.8	225.1	229.6	238.1	8.3	4.5	0.3	1.5	2.0	4.0
(c) Electricity	236.8	257.0	269.9	288.8	311-7	9.0	7.8	8.5	5.0	7.0	1.6

Govt. Monopolies—Need Restructuring

The policy of reserving too many industries for the public sector, though well intentioned, proved to be disastrous. Consider this example. Today POSCO of S. Korea is the world's largest steel plant. In the 1950s S. Korea didn't produce any steel at all but was importing steel from India. India's 'TATA Steel' was at that time producing tonnes of steel. TATA Steel which had the resources and competence to grow fast was denied permission to expand in spite of its repeated requests because steel was in the reserved category. Over the years the public sector steel plants also couldn't grow fast enough because of resource constraints. The consequence is that India's steel plants are by International standards obsolete and inefficient.

Monopolies—A Distorted Definition

Perhaps India alone has the dubious distinction in the world of having given a perverted definition of monopoly. Obsessed by socialism and in the missionary zeal to achieve an equitable and just society we defined a monopoly as one with an asset of Rs.10 crores (1969). Subsequently this was raised to Rs.100 crores in 1985. In this age of mega corporations and capital intensive sophisticated technology Rs.100 crores is a small amount. The world would not have benefited from General Motors, IBM (USA), Siemens, BASF (Germany), Honda, Sony (Japan), Hyundai, Samsung (S. Korea), etc. had their respective countries followed a restrictive industrial policy like our own MRTP Act. Unfortunately we took too long to learn from mistakes. In the early 1980s when there was cement scarcity in the country and when cement was sold by traders at high prices in the black markets, repeated requests by ACC, India's largest cement manufacturer to increase capacity was turned down because it was an MRTP Company.

The amendment of the MRTP Act as per new Industrial policy removes this distortion.

Thus the fact is that successive industrial policies, though with good intentions created many distortions in our industrial system.

Govt's Role has to be Regulatory, in India it Proved to be Restrictive

The new policy which aims at dismantling this restrictive control machanism can be expected to 'uncage the tiger'.

DEFICIENCIES AND WEAKNESSES

Though a substantial improvement over previous policies, the new Policy suffers from some deficiencies and weaknesses which can be summarised as follows :

1. *Privatisation is being perused as a half-hearted measure :*

Disinvestment of govt. equity is used more as a revenue raising measure than as an attempt toprofessionalise the management of PSUs.

2. *Lacklustre Performance in Financial Sector Reforms*

In fact financial sector reforms should precede industrial reforms.

3. An exit policy is hanging fire for too long a time.

4. A sensible drug policy is yet to be finalised.

5. Reduction in fiscal deficit and import compression caused by depreciation of rupees following convertibility have led to industrial recession especially in areas like automobiles, steel, petroleum, etc. This problem needs urgent attention.

Conclusion

The economic survey 1993-94 indicates that further reforms in the industrial policy are on the anvil, especially in the area of Procedures and Constraints affecting project implementation. It had also been decided to shift the base year of the Index of Industrial Production from 1980-81 to 1985-86 in view of the need to improve the methodology and data-base for estimating the Index of Industrial Production. It is further estimated that the Industrial growth rate is 2.7 percent from July to October 1993. The direct foreign investment is also showing strong positive response to structural reforms. The actual inflow of investment from 1991 to October 1993 stands at Rs. 25.68 billions.

Undoubtedly the policy of liberalisation and globalisation is on the right track. We are moving along with the international trend. The beneficial results have shown a quantum jump. The total FDI approvals during 1975-90 were only worth Rs. 1,300 crores. i.e. an annual average of only around Rs. 87 crores. As against this the post-policy approvals have really taken off to Rs. 1,950 crores between August. 1991 and July 1992 and further Rs. 7,220 crores between August.1992 and July 1993. The fact that FDI approvals for the first seven months of this year at Rs. 4,880 crores are 40 times the total FDI approvals in whole of 1990 at Rs. 120 crores is an indicator of the shape of things to come.

The 'Economist' described India as a 'caged Tiger' with a potential to leap like the Asian Tigers. Dismantling the cage built with licences, permits, quotas, MRTP, FERA, etc. has started off well but is by no means complete. 'Tigerisation' of the economy needs more steps like the following:

1. Speeding up the financial sector reforms.
2. An exit policy with reasonable safeguards.
3. Tackling recession with further cuts in lending rates.

Implementation of the above measures along with other measures in the package will certainly speed up industrialisation in our economy which has already turned the corner. What is required is the political will to continue with the reforms and implement reforms which might be politically unpopular in the short run.

Reference

1. E.P.W. June 30, 1990.
2. E.P.W. March 16, 1994.
3. World Development Report 1993.
4. Human Development Report 1993.
5. Government of India C.S.O. (Various Years).
6. Economic Survey, Govt. of India 1993, 1994.
7. R.B.I. Bulletin, January 1992.
8. Yojana, September 15, 1991.
9. Centre for monitoring Indian Economy (Various years).

2

UNSUSTAINABLE GLOBALISATION A THEORETICAL-CUM-HISTORICAL PERSPECTIVE

*Dr. M. Kunhaman**

Once, it was thought that 'plan' and 'market' were mutually exclusive. To ask for a system characterised by the co-existence of the two was considered analogous to asking for a 'hot ice cream'. This was the position taken by the French philosopher Saint Simon in the early nineteenth century. According to Marx and Engels, market (commodity) economy was the centrepiece of a class society.

Maurice Dobb maintained in the sixties of this century that planning was the essential integrating mechanism under socialism in place of the market mechanism which was the nerve-fibre of a capitalist economy.[1] Under a market system, economics dominates politics while under planning, politics dominates economics.

Thus, till recently, we were more familiar with the usage plan *versus* market. Today, such terms as "market socialism", "socialist commodity production"[2], etc., have become popular. Plan and market are no longer considered as incongruous. Perhaps the most glaring instance in this regard is India where even as the country is undergoing an irreversible structural adjustment, the government continues to harp on planning. Speaking about the "avoidable tragedy of the Indian left", Pranab Bardhan maintains that "one can have planning and still use market signals in implementing the plan. This is the essence of market socialism."[3]

* Reader, Dept. of Economics, University of Kerala.

It is instructive to note that the shift in focus from the usage 'plan *versus* market' to the usage 'plan and market' represents a radical change in economic thinking and socialist practice. Before we discuss this radical change, however, let us make the conceptual issues clear.

While conceding that no system ever existed in its prestine purity so as to enable an empirical observer to discern its characteristic components in an unambiguous fashion, it is nevertheless, essential to delineate these components as an epistemological prerequisite to developing the thought process. Further, since the issues involved are relevant from the praxiological and policy points of view, the need for such a delineation becomes all the greater.

Semantically, the terms market and plan, poles apart, represent two discrete and mutually opposing systems. Market implies a class society. Hence, it may be specifically noted that while market outside capitalism is quite conceivable, capitalism sans market is inconceivable. It is true that in almost all pre-capitalist formations, market had existed in one form or another and serving different purposes, Karl Polyani speaks about the redistributive function of the market in tribal societies. Being self-replacing and self-producing, such societies, based as they were on the principle of equity required the disposal within themselves the surplus that occurred from time to time. Polyani emphasises the point that the market was embedded in the social institutions and was never used for acquisitive purposes. And the occurrence of the surplus, rather than the outcome of deliberate actions, was mere happenstance.

In peasant societies, the surplus was deliberately created. Its emergence was necessitated either by fixed cash requirement (for instance, payment of rent or tribute in cash) or by the desire to buy non-farm goods. The first created the proverbial negative market response of the peasants while the second accentuated the process of class formation through the differentiation of the peasantry. The differentiation, fuelled by the market, inevitably leads to the polarisation of the society into the proletariat and the bourgeoisie. It needs to be stressed here that from commercialisation (i.e., marketisation of the kind elaborated in this para) to capitalism, it was only a short step. Thus, the unavoidable culmination is the emergence of capitalist relations. The classic illustration of this process is provided by Lenin in the Development of Capitalism in Russia whose central theme is the examination of the process formation of a home market for Russian Capitalism.[4]

What makes capitalism inseparable from market is the fact that while surplus value is created in production, it has to be realised through exchange, i.e., through the market. The exhaustion of their domestic market prompted the pioneering industrial nations to conquer other nations and convert them into markets for their products, thus leading to imperialism. The scramble for markets among the imperial powers resulted in wars. Thus, market and capitalism are inseparable. Capitalism, in its highest form, cannot exist without imperialism. And imperialism inevitably leads to war. These are not only theoretical speculations or possibilities but concrete historical experiences.[5]

To do justice to the history of economic ideas, it must be mentioned that Adam Smith, the father of economics science, and more systematically and elaborately, Ricardo, dwelt on these lines, though purely' economistically. Smith in particular originated the idea that economic growth depends upon division of labour and specialisation which, in their turn, depend upon the size of the market. Market, in order words, was considered as the engine of growth. For the expansion of the market, *laissez faire* domestically and free trade internationally were advocated. However, Smith did not visualise or dilate on the frictions that might be potentially or actually created in the wake of market expansion. What needs special emphasis in this connection is the fact that market, especially for Smith, spontaneously evolved and resulted in the all round social benefit. This way of looking at the market, while perfectly in tune with the naturalism and optimism of Smith, is nonetheless lopsided as it ignores the innumerable undersirable consequences of market expansions; consequences to which the hitherto World history bears ample testimony.

Conventional wisdom says that market promotes competition and efficiency and hereby economic growth. This wisdom which has been handed down through generations is contained in the books in mainstream economics whose analytical fulcrum is the market. It may be remembered in this context that the new science of economics is mythology. It mythifies the processes and realities of life. Its edifice crumbles the moment its assumptions are questioned. Many an abstract and illogical mind in the profession has found easy refuge in the conundrum, *ceteris paribus*. The most typical case is the theory of the market. It is doubtful whether perfect competition, an academic myth reigning supreme in the world of economic thinking, ever existed in the history of mankind. The hitherto global economic history indisputably shows that free market capitalism has led to monopoly, oligopoly and imperialism. The 'qualities' of competition and efficiency remain confined to the better-off fringe of the society. In a class society free competition is, in fact, the very negation of democracy and equity, for natural justice requires that competition should be not only free but also fair. Competition among unequals can be neither free nor fair. Hence, the so-called free society which is said to be the concomitant of the market economy is an optical illusion created and maintained by the ruling class to keep the oppressed sections of society silenced. The concept of free competition sounds hollow and meaningless for "the oppressed two-thirds of mankind".[6] comprising groups like the blacks of Africa, the impoverished Indians of Latin America and the *dalits* and *adivasis* of India.

Again, the notion that a capitalist society ensures the full development of the productive forces is not substantiated either theoretically or historically. Theoretically speaking, it is in the interest of a capitalist to restrict the output and create artificial scarcity so as to jack up prices and make higher profits. Hence, unemployment of labour and underutilisation of capital at any point in time are the characteristic features of a market economy. The tendency among the Indian industrialists to corner industrial licences and build excess productive capacities is too well known to need corroboration.

Besides, in a capitalist economy, what is produced is not at all important. How much is produced is the overwhelming consideration. In other words, such a country tries to maximise the growth rate unmindful of the composition of the social product. Leading industrial countries like America produce armament goods and highly toxical goods; export these to the third world countries and import healthy products from the latter. The new ideas of free trade, global market integration and liberalisation are subtle and surreptitious attempts to distort and deform the economics of the third world countries which had become, since the second World War, conscious of the necessity and desirability for traversing a self-reliant growth path and maintaining political sovereignty. In other words, these are nothing but glittering wrappers for neocolonial gadgets of exploitation.

Moreover, the unbridled and ruthless pursuit of profit-maxmisation has been quenched at the heavy cost of environmental degradation. Air and water get increasingly contaminated. There is reckless utilisation of non-renewable resources. The social cost of capitalist production has amassed devastating proportions. The silver-lining, however, is that progressive opinion the world over is clamouring for sustainable development.

It is true that the market provides incentives for production. Man needs externally infused motivation to overcome lethargy and inertia which are inherent in him. Man's natural tendency is to remain idle. Overcoming idleness requires deliberate effort. Of course, man responds to external stimuli. Various systems provide various stimuli. A market system provides material stimulus; and material stimulus only. Poan Robinson spoke about the "animal spirit"[7] which is the motivational force of a capitalist. A capitalist is aggressive and profit-minded. What happens to the society in general as a result of his pursuit of aggrandisement is never his concern. This is because no noble ideology or moral principle underlies such a system.

From the foregoing discussion on the evolution and functioning of the market economy, a few points stand out prominently. They are the following:

1. Market as an institution emerged spontaneously.
2. In whatever social formation it emerged, it soon gave rise to a class society. A free market in a classless society is a contradiction in terms.
3. A market economy is characterised by the existence of economic inequalities, exploitation and oppression. It leads to the increasing misery of the majority and the ever fattening of an affluent fringe.
4. The belief that the market *ipso facto* promotes competition, efficiency and growth is a myth. In fact, the inevitable results of the operation of the market are unemployment, monopoly/oligopoly and restriction of output. It also gives rise to imperialism and war.
5. Market as an institution or mechanism never had an ideological/moral underpinning.
6. Market has given rise to such undesirable tendencies as to pose a threat to the existence of the capitalist system itself.

The system hedges against the threat through devising and maintaining an elaborate system of social security.

7. Thus, the Smithian belief of 'naturalism' and 'optimism' (according to which economic institutions are supposed to spontaneously emerge and whatever institutions so emerge are supposed to be socially beneficial) does not hold in the case of market as an institution.

One would, rightly, think that, theoretically and historically, it was the unwholsome tendencies of the market system that gave rise to the emergence and increasing popularity of the planning system, for it was thought that those tendencies were the outcome of the chaotic and uncoordinated functioning of the various components of a private enterprise system. Co-ordination eliminates chaos. Unlike the developed market economies which 'grow' (note that the text-book distinction between growth and development is highly relevant here) spontaneously, a socialist economy plans its development. The former never had any unified goal. Whatever they achieved is the unintended outcome of disparate, spontaneous actions. Whereas a socialist society cannot leave things to chance and await and accept spontaneous, unintended results. Socialism is not a spontaneous evolution. It is the outcome of purposeful actions by bold individuals infused with imagination and new values. The basic philosophy governing socialist action is that man is not merely a creation but also the creator of history. He creates history. It was stated way back in 1845 by Marx in the Thesis on Feuerbach that "The philosophers have only interpreted the world in various ways; the point, however, is to change it."[8] In other words, the bedrock of communism is the belief that man is the architect of his own destiny. Communist philosophy is addressed to the oppressed telling them point blank that though their underdog position is the creation of the oppressor, their emancipation is possible only for themselves. It is pointless to either remain helpless and passive or to expect a saviour.

A socialist society is a classless society established after a class struggle. Such a society requires a plan which is the substitute for the market in a capitalist society. Planning means coordination and centralisation. The very precondition for centralised planning is the social ownership of the means of production. A socialist economy can never afford to aim exclusively at the maximisation of the rate of growth of national output regardless of the composition of that output. In such an economy, what is produced is perhaps more important than how much is produced. It cannot countenance unequal distribution of income and wealth. Its purpose is concrete and systemic, viz., to maximise welfare on an equitable basis. The promotion of welfare is not confined to the people of the particular socialist country in question; rather, the welfare of the working class in the entire world is its concern. It needs to be specially noted that the socialist countries never tried to establish and exploit colonies.

Unlike in a market economy, in a socialist economy, there is no alienation of the producer from the means of production. The producer is fully aware that the society which he has *created* owns the means of production and are used for the reconstruction of the society to which he is committed.

The question of incentives under a planned regime assumes great importance here. It is widely held that a socialist economy does not provide adequate incentives for effort, enterprise and incentives despite the fact that Oskar Lange and Fred M. Taylor dismissed that view as "folklore" in 1938.[9] For a socialist, his social commitment, rather than material incentive, is the driving force. He is an ideologically conditioned individual. He is the architect of a socialist society. Morally, he is on a higher plane.

Till 1917, socialism was considered to be an Utopian idea. But with the establishment of the USSR, it became a practicable one. Similarly, till 1928, planning was not regarded as a workable proposition. However, in 1928, that impression disappeared. No wonder, from the late twenties onwards, the entire world rivetted its attention on the USSR to see how that country, based as it was on the three core pillars, viz, socialism, Planning and single-party rule, was going to perform. It was soon proved that it was only the socialist system which was able to remain insulated from the economic crisis that engulfed the entire capitalist world in the thirties and also that basic problems like poverty, shelter and illiteracy of the general masses could be solved within a short period only under socialism. More importantly, thanks to Stalin who elevated some of the persons belonging to the lowest rungs of the pre-Revolution Russia to important positions both in the Party and in the Government, thinking of the entire society underwent a radical change. It shook the former ruling class from its smug belief that only it could rule. It also shook the vast masses of the oppressed sections from their fatalistic belief that they were destined perpetually to be ruled. The oppressed the world over began to have courage and a new outlook. In their initial, justified enthusiasm, the formerly exploited sections in Soviet Russia went about reconstructing their society in the course of which they were bound to take certain drastic steps which, in the eyes of the former ruling classes in all countries, were excesses and for which the latter unjustifiably blamed Stalin exclusively. Similar things were later to happen in the tiny State of Kerala in the sub-continental country that is India. In this tiny State, the exploited class, the vast majority of it belonging to lower castes, created history by catapulting to power a Communist Government through the accepted procedures of an electoral democracy. The oppressed sections got a unique and unprecedented opportunity to come to power. They boldly went about , reconstructing their society. Their unbounded enthusiasm pervaded all levels of society. Consequently, the communal-capitalist-feudal elements constituting the former ruling class colluded and succeeded in toppling a constitutionally formed State Government through blatantly undemocratic and unconstitutional means. None the less, the communal-capitalist-feudal combine could not prevent the spread of communist ideology in the State, Instead, the ideology spread far and wide. It may be noted that the CPI (M) is the only major communist party in the world today which is growing even as it tenaciously sticks to basic tenets of Marxism-Leninism. This is due to its appeal to the lower castes and classes. Of all the political parties in India, it can claim the back-up of the largest number of intellectuals in the country. For it, concepts such as class struggle 'people's democracy' and proletarian internationalism are not "major obsessions" as Nilanjan Mukhopadhyay thinks,[10] but are articles of faith and guiding principles. Its secular credentials are unquestioned. Its leaders who formed governments in various states have a clean track record. Even their arch enemies do not accuse them of corruption and malpractices. No wonder, even the rightist and centrist parties in India are emulating the style of functioning (including the language) of the communist leaders.

Something can be seen in South Africa, another country with a large communist party still sticking to the ideology of Marxism-Leninism. The African National Congress which, under the irrepressible Nelson Mandela, is waging a life-and-death battle against the apartheid state is readily getting the ideological support of the Communist Party in the country.

It may be emphasised at this stage that the attempt here is not to imply that everything was quite good in the former Soviet Union or any other socialist country. Before we dilate on the relevant historical dimensions, it is incumbent upon us to set the theoretical perspective so as to clear the cobwebs from our frame of thinking. Marx himself did not say much about the functioning of a post-revolutionary society. He was more concerned about the law of motion of a modern capitalist society. Regarding the post- revolutionary society, he, however, gave a warning. In such a society, the class forces would not be absent, they would be only dormant. They would ever try for dominance. This called for eternal vigilance on the part of the working class lest the bourgeois elements should come to the fore and consequently the classless society would relapse into a class society.

In fact, even today, our knowledge of the history of socialist societies is woefully limited. The renowned historian, Irfan Habib, in his V.P. Chintan Memorial Lecture delivered in Madras in 1988, categorically stated that "one of the admitted weaknesses of Marxist historiography lies in the limitations of its analysis of the history of socialist societies, whose existence began with the Russian Revolution of 1917. While in Marx's Capital, we have theoretical framework for understanding the laws of motion of capitalist society, no such framework is available for socialism... Not until 1952 did the Soviet Union possess in Stalin's pamphlet, Economic Problems of Socialism in the USSR, an authoritative exposition of some of the most elementary questions relating to socialist economy. But Stalin left many important problems unresolved or omitted them from view altogether."[11] It may be noted that this serious lacuna in our understanding of post-revolutionary societies was filled to a great extent by Paual M. Sweezy through his book, Post-Revolutionary Society, published in 1980. The central observation of Sweezy is highly relevant in the present context. According to him what was important was not the elimination of "all manifestations of capitalist behaviour patterns" from the socialist economies but the fact that those patterns had "ceased to *dominate* the functioning of the economy and hence, indirectly, to shape the objectives and tasks of political power. In capitalist society, the state is the servant of the economy; in Soviet type societies, it is the master."[12]

However, it was Mao Tse Dong who most cogently prescribed the prerequisites for making the socialist system an on-going one. He rightly emphasised the need for eliminating the gaps between manual labour and intellectual labour, and rural society and urban society. A post- revolutionary society needs a permanent cultural revolution.

In the former USSR and East European countries, however, a permanent cultural revolution did not take place. Rather, the post-Stalin period witnessed the hypertrophy of the bureaucratic machinery. Planning came to be regarded as synonymous with the public sector. The bureaucracy, party as well as official, became a class into itself claiming special rights and cornering privileges. A stage was reached when the party moved away from the people and the leaders became inaccessible to the people. The August 1991 Putsch in the then Soviet Russia was proof enough that the socialist elements were still vigilant in that country and would reassert at the appropriate time. Gorbachev who, by digging his own grave, would find a position in the annals of history as the most myopic leader the world has ever seen, was not able to realise that fact.

Now, coming to the first part of our title, viz., "Plan and Market". It is true that Marx maintained that market economy (read the capitalist economy) had witnessed the greatest development of the productive forces. By this, however, he did not mean that full development of productive forces is not possible in a socialist economy. What he actually meant was that a capitalist economy registers higher growth of the productive forces than the pre-capitalist social formation. Though he did not explicitly state the superiority of the socialist system over the market system with regard to the growth of the productive forces, by his assumption that each successive mode of production represents a higher social order, he, in fact, very much meant it.

However, it must be remembered that the efficacy of the capitalist methods (distinct from the capitalist relations) was recognised by Lenin himself. That is why rather than straight-away removing the market after the October Revolution, he opted for the New Economic Policy (1921 to 1928) which placed great reliance on the market system.[13]

Whatever assessment of Stalin may be done today with the advantage of hindsight, it is an incontrovertible fact that he had to undertake the unenviable task of taking the Soviet economy from lower level socialism to higher level socialism. What the Soviet Union had already achieved was only socialism; economic development was yet to take place. And economic development, irrespective of the nature of the system, requires, as a precondition, the generation and mobilisation of social surplus for reinvestment. This necessitated drastic actions like collectivisation. Through planning, the Soviet economy was able to realise amazing results. Marshall Goldman gave in 1968 a succint account of the Soviet achievements. He said, "....the Russians have become the world's second largest industrial power. If any thing their heavy industrial sector is overdeveloped. With such a solid industrial structure, it stands to reason that the Russians have also been able to produce some sophisticated equipment. To any one who has followed their space exploits, this is clear. As the years go by, it becomes more difficult to recapture the panic that prevailed in the West when the Russians sent the world's first Sputnik skyward in 1957. Yuri Gagarin's manned flight a few years later did nothing to dispel this hysteria. Comparable American space achievements lagged two or three years behind for what seemed to be a depressingly long period of time. Throughout the period, it became clear to all but the most dogmatic skeptics that the Russians had attained an impressive mastery over science and technology... In 1957, we had more to steal from the Russians than they had to steal from us."[14]

Unsurprisingly, when the former colonies, after gaining political independence since the second World War, began to engage in the reconstruction of their economies, they had no doubt whatsoever as regards the method of attaining growth with justice. They took to planning like ducks to water. The Soviet Union readily came to their assistance by way of moral, ideological and economic support and guidance. Nehru, the architect of Indian planning and the unflinching votary of the public sector, was greatly impressed by the Soviet gains under planning (That he could not imbibe the true socialist spirit is a different matter altogether).

Even some of the classical capitalist countries began to adopt and apply planning technics. It needs special mention that planning technics like PERT and CPM are very systematically used in the United States. In point of fact, as Amit Bhaduri rightly observes, all the present-day capitalist economies are 'mixed' economies in varying proportions. "A totally free enterprise market economy without any role for the state is merely an ideological abstraction far removed from the reality of capitalism."[15] The age of *laissez faire* has long gone and for ever.

When the developing countries, through a planned regime, began to show tendencies for self-reliant growth and when they began to assert in world bodies like the UNO, the mandarins of the capitalist order became jittery and started reining them through conditionalities attached to the loans advanced by the IMF and world Bank as well as by individual countries. These conditionalities consist mainly of the following:

1. Privatisation.
2. Elimination of subsidies of all kinds.
3. Curtailment of budgetary provision for welfare programmes.
4. Liberalisation.
5. Glohalisation.

The mesmerizing words are 'liberalisation', and 'market-friendly approach'.

Michael Choussudovsky opined recently that by accepting these conditionalities the "debtor countries forgo economic sovereignty and control over fiscal and monetary policy.... Debt management policies by creditor nations and institutions are thus used to 'remould' Third World economies since they constitute through IMF and World Bank Policy conditionality, the basis for 'appropriately' redirecting the macro economic policy of individual (indebted) countries."[16] A paradox should also be noted here. The policies which the debtor countries are forced to adopt under duress by the capitalist countries are not adopted by the latter themselves. They are adopting more and more protective policies. The paradox becomes even clearer in the case of subsidies. Abolition of subsidies is insisted upon by the developed capitalist countries even as the agricultural sector in Germany, France, Britain, Iceland and other West European countries and also in North America depends on "gigantic subsidies."[17]

The Third World ruling classes which, both in their tastes and outlook, are akin more to their counterparts in the capitalist countries than to the masses of either their own or of the capitalist countries fall an easy prey to these conditionalities and avoid reorganisation of their economies and polity which may endanger their privileged position. The most glaring example in this regard is India where the Central Government, through a well known economist, Manmohan Singh, is planning for chaos. Already, Kenneth Gallerith had characterised India as "a functioning anarchy". The

Quixotic policies of our present-day rulers give the impression that they are converting India into a 'non-functioning anarchy'. What innocent Gorbachev and cunning Yeltsin achieved in the former Soviet Union holds out a serious lesson for us. On the economic front, what was once the Soviet Union, has not heralded complete marketisation. What has been achieved is chaos. On the political front, however, the actions of Gorbachev and Yeltsin have resulted in the disintegration of the Soviet Union which once served as the symbol of humanity's new vision. In India, let us hope that the wayward policies of the ruling class will not result in the disintegration of the nation.

True, in the former Soviet Union and the East European countries, with the disappearance of the central authority and the command system, the importance of planning has declined. However, as of now, planning has not entirely been replaced by the market. In the place of the changed system, what system will finally emerge is quite unpredictable. The uneasy combination of plan and market cannot exist for long. The market phenomenon, once started, will pick up its own momentum. It may not stop midway. If it continues uninterruptedly, there will be class differentiation and the eventual emergence of a bipolar society of the exploiters and the exploited. Will the pro-socialist forces, the oppressed of the world, allow such a denouement? That is the million dollar question.

References

1. Maurice Dobb in the "Introductory Note" in Mikhail Bor, Aims and Methods of Soviet Planning, Lawrence and Wishart, London, 1967.
2. Yugoslav top economist "B. Kedrick coined the term Socialist commodity Production"See Debora D. Milen Kovitch, Plan and Market in Yugoslav Economic Thought, Yale University Press 1971, Review by Carmelo Mesa-Lago in Economic Development and Cultural Change, January 1973.
3. Pranab Bardhan. "Avoidable Tragedy of the Left in India" *Economic and Political Weekly* (EPW, hereafter), October 19, 1991. For a detailed discussion on market socialism, see Alec Nove, Political Economy of Soviet Socialism, George Allen & Unwin, 1979, especially chapter 7, "Market Socialism and its Critics".
4. V.I. Lenin, The Development of Capitalism in Russia, Progress Publishers, Moscow, 1956, Preface to the First Edition.
5. Paul A. Baran, "The Political Economy of Growth, Penguin Books, 1957, Chapter 1, "A General Overview".

6. Amiya Kumar Bagchi, "Historicising the Problems of Socialism", *Social Scientist* No. 185, October 1988.
7. Poan Robinson "Model of Accomodation" in A.K. Sen, (ed.) Growth Economics, Penguin Books, 1971.
8. K. Marx, Theses on Feuerbach, XI, 1845 in K. Marx and F. Engels, Selected Works, Foreign Languages Publishing House, Moscow, 1951, vol. 2, P. 367.

3

THE WORLD ECONOMIC ORDER : THE PAST AND THE EMERGING TRENDS

(Prof. (Dr.) K. Ramachandran Nair,
Head,Department of Economics,
University of Kerala.)

The World Order that was created at the end of the Second World War was essentially based on bipolarity of the USA and USSR, the two superpowers and the dominance of security issues. The result was the creation of systematic structures and alliances which defined the international environment. The ideological dimension contained in the bipolar rivalry was obvious as the USA espoused democracy, capitalism and a market system, while the USSR embodied totalitarian politics, socialism and a centralised planned/command economy. The third world countries which emerged in the process of decolonisation were be wildered by the bipolarity. Some liked to come closer to USA or USSR while a few adopted a neutral stand. But soon both the superpowers realised that one quick way to gain friends in the Third World is to offer financial as well as technological support for the development of the Third World countries. The USA in particular, besides offering massive support on their own, tried to use the multilateral institutions like the IMF and IBRD to her advantage. But since this entailed unilateral defending of the value of the US dollar which was functioning more or less as an international medium of exchange facilitating global trade and commerce, it added to the burden on the US economy in terms of huge fiscal and balance of payments deficits. It is in this context that by 1971-73 the US announced its decision to end its unilateral commitment to defend the dollar and function as the locomotive for the global economy. The USA then wanted trilateral coordination among the USA, Europe and Japan for global economic management. But this kind of trilateralism seems to have broken down in the late 1970s when the USA again asserted its unilateral role by pulling the world economy out of the 1980-82 recession at the cost of huge fiscal and balance of payments deficits.

The shift in the US policy, however, did not last long. In the Plaza Accord, an attempt was made to put trilateral co-ordination back into the forefront of world economic management. The Plaza Accord called for Japan and Germany to expand their domestic economies and assume greater global responsibilities while the USA shifted from *debt-led growth* to *export-led growth*. The logic of the Plaza Accord was to convert the US deficits through export-led growth. For this the USA should pursue a global economic policy to secure greater access to world markets for its goods, investment and services. This explains the US interest in getting the Uruguay Round of multilateral trade negotiations concluded at an early date. The USA also decided to put pressure on its trading partners to remove whatever barriers that existed on the movement of US goods, investment and services. Though it may help the USA, will it help to provide an adequate frame-work for sustainable world economic growth?

The third world countries were watching the shifts in the global economic policy of the USA. Soon they discovered the ground realities of the politics of foreign trade and foreign aid. They became aware of the tragic consequences of trade among unequal partners and the inequities that are built into the global economic order. The secular deterioration in terms of trade put a brake on the development of third world countries. The centre-periphery nexus was getting strengthened in the global enonomy. An effort was made by the third world countries to form groups and forge alliances like the UNCTAD and Group of 77. They demanded level playing ground, and non-discriminatory rules for international economic relations and a more equitable New International Economic Order (NIEO). When the Third World united to fight for their rights, the rich industrial countries decided to counter the move by forming the G-7 and using the IMF and IBRD to put pressure on the Third World to change their policies which would help the rich further.

The IMF and IBRD, the multilateral institutions, ceased to be multilateral when they began to dance to the tune called by the USA and its G-7 allies. The outcome of this is well explained by the Report of the South Commission, authored by no less a person than Dr. Manmohan Singh, the Union Finance Minister of India who paradoxically is now the most articulate spokesman for the IMF-IBRD medicine for developing countries. The Report says:

> ``Developed countries were able to use the international financial institutions to impose their views on the third world countries and at the same time to demand that the latter should adjust their economies through contradictory policies. This was a form of neò-colonialism. The debt crisis was used by the North as an opportunity to influence their domestic choices and to, impose on them externally determined values, policies, concessions and patterns of development ... The Social and political costs of inappropriate measures were then paid by the victim countries and their peoples and any resulting instability was used by the North as a further opportunity for external intervention ... The establishment of a system of international economic relations in which the South's Second class status would be institutionalised is an imminent danger."

The above picture is corroborated by Davison L. Budhoo, the economist from Grenada who resigned from the IMF and registered his feelings in a letter to Camdessus, the Managing Director of the IMF. He wrote thus:

> "I resigned from the staff of the IMF after 12 years and after 1000 days of official Fund Work, *hawking* your medicines and your bag of tricks to governments and to peoples in Latin America and the Caribbean and Africa. To me, resignation is a priceless liberation for which I have taken the first big step to that place where I may hope to wash my hands off what in my mind is blood of millions of poor and starving peoples. Mr. Camdessus, the blood is so much, you know it *runs* in rivers. It dries up too, it cakes all over me; sometimes I feel that there is not enough soap in the whole world to *cleanse* me from the things I did in your name and in the name of your predecessors and your official seal...... You will have to reply, because the *charges* that I make are not light charges—they are *charges* that touch at the very heart of Western Society, and Western

> morality and post-war inter-governmental institutionalism that have degenerated into fake and sham, under the pretext of establishing and maintaining international economic and global efficiency".

The IMF, to quote Lawrence Surendra, has virtually become an agent of powerful shareholders, USA and its G-7 allies being the largest among them. The developing countries, therefore, feel that such an institution cannot be timely international in its character and functioning. The challenging task before them is to resist such policies and medicines that are prescribed by the IMF and IBRD which, in the long run, would impose on them alien and inappropriate patterns of development.

Now fifty years after the IMF and the IBRD, the Bretton Woods twins, were born, the global economy has entered an era dramatically different from anything it has experienced so far. The era of Cold War has ended. Germany is unified, but the escalating costs of unification (expected to reach 150 billion dollars in 1994) and of aid to Eastern Europe and the former Soviet Union have created a large budget deficit and the risk of inflation. To cut the deficit, it spends less and economic growth in Germany slows down considerably. Germany in the 1990s has started exporting slow growth and recession. Under the rules of the European Monetary System, the other European countries have had no choice but to follow suit. The European Community has become stronger with the emergence of Fortress Europe, thereby causing a serious threat to the hegemony of the USA.This threat has been further strengthened by Japan, the East Asian Superpower. Though Japan became a net importer of Capital, its trade surplus has been expanding creating problems for its trading partners, particularly the USA. This may lead to USA and Japan heading for a new confrontation on trade. The possibility of an emerging two-front trade war between USA and European Union and between USA and Japan cannot be ruled out. The USA has already threatened Japan with action under Special 301 and Super 301 if the latter does not open its domestic market for US Motorola's Cellular Phones. If USA, Europe and Japan fight with each other, who will take on the responsibility of functioning as a useful locomotive for global economic growth? Can the G-7 group undertake this responsibility collectively? But no country in this group is today free from problems of deficits and stagflation. All of them want to sell in world markets in order to give a boost to their sagging domestic economices. For this they advocate globalisation of the economies of the developing countries and greater access to these new markets.

The spirit of multilateralism is now threatened by growing regionalism as evidenced by the European Union, the North American Free Trade Association (NAFTA), the Malaysian proposal in setting up an East Asian Caucus and Asia Pacific Economic Community (APEC). USA still continues its single track, multitrack and fast track approach to global economic relations. Under the single track approach it has made it clear that it would be free to use the provisions of the U.S Omnibus Trade Act and take action under Special 301 and Super 301 if any country's policies are considered as unfair to US trade interests and thus US will continue to support unilateral action. Under the multi-track approach US would be free to enter into bilateral arrangements with other nations to protect its self-interest. Multilateralism is recognised only under the fast track approach in the global economic policy of the US. The above analysis would give the impression that the US would give top priority to unilateralism in order to protect its self-interest and in the process would pressurise and terrorise other countries with retaliatory measures.

More and more among the developing countries who are struggling with large fiscal and balance of payment deficits and external liabilities have now been asked by the IMF and IBRD to adopt fiscal correction, fiscal consolidation, medium term economic stabilisation and longterm structural adjustment with thrust on privatisation, liberalisation and globalisation. As mentioned earlier the US and the G-7 group of countries are using the IMF and IBRD in supporting US portion on Special 301, Super 301, Nuclear Non-Proliferation Treaty (NPT), Missile Technology Control Regime (MTCR), Multilateral Investment Guarantee Agency (MIGA) Convention, the Dunkel Proposals, Human Rights etc. and link them up with the domestic economic management of developing countries. The USA wants to protect its hegemony and retain its superpower status by keeping the emerging global economic order as unjust and inequitous as it was since the second World War and till the end of the 1980s.

The emerging global economic order seems to have entered unchartered turbulent waters without compass, captain or engine. What would be the possible outcome? *In Europe,* the East European countries belonging to the former Warsaw Pact may prefer to come closer to the European Community and sign association agreements with member countries. Baltic states and other republics which arose from the ashes of the USSR may also seek membership of the European Union, since Russia itself is moving closer to it. *In Asia* a Pan-Asian grouping based on the Malaysian proposal for East Asian Economic Caucus may bring together former adversaries like China, Vietnam and Korea together. *In Latin America,* a similar trend may emerge with new sub-regional pacts like Southern Cone Common Market and a revitalised Andean Pact. The NAFTA has become a reality. Attempts may be made to expand the NAFTA so as to create a bigger and most powerful Western Hemisphere Free Trade Area (WHTFA). Even India has been advised by J. Bhagwati and T. N. Srinivasan to join the NAFTA to take advantage from the global market. With the thrust on globalisation and marketisation many countries have started adopting their own versions of market economics. In most of these countries a debate is likely to take place on whether their decision to adopt a market economy would magically solve their basic problems of poverty and under-development. The consensus that seems most probable to emerge out of this debate is that neither the State nor the Market, on its own, can solve, the above problems and what is needed is to retain both State and Market and make them work better through a mutually supporting and reinforcing relationship.

In the emerging global economic order, as we visualise it, we need to think about certain fundamental issues.

(1) Re-examine the implications of the principles of Non-Discrimination, National Treatment and Unconditional Most Favoured Nation Treatment in the context of replacing the GATT by the New World Trade Organisation (WTO). Under National Treatment standard, countries reciprocate in applying the same laws and regulations to the goods and firms of other countries as they do to their own. Under conditional MFN, countries that extend special favours to one of their trading partners must extend the same favours to all. That system is based on the premise that its members pursue similar objective in a similar way.

(2) We need to develop a mutually acceptable mechanism for harmonisation of domestic economic policies among both

rich and poor countries for promoting global economic integration. As a first step in this direction, smooth relations among the big powers should be ensured.

(3) We need to evolve and operationalise a global collective approach to tackle emerging global issues like energy, environmental degradation, global warming, protection of bio-diversity, arms trade, drug traffic, international terrorism etc. which are going to be much more complex than issues like fiscal and balance of payment deficits, exchange rate instability and inflation. Can the above emerging issues be resolved by entrusting the task to the G-7 countries or the P-7 countries (Security Council members numbering 5 and Japan and Germany added).

(4) The record of G-7, IMF, IBRD, GATT, UNCTAD etc. need to be reassessed in the light of the evidence on their inability to check currency misalignments, trade imbalances, international supercycle of debt, financial mania, and recurrent recession and stagflation in global economy.

All countries, rich and poor, now live in a highly interdependent world of pluralistic power configuration/network. In it they have almost lost their real sovereignty over their own affairs. Who will take the initiative to create systemic structures for forging collective leadership in ensuring a stable equitable global political and economic order? If we fail in this, there may emerge strong hostile regional blocs that would become increasingly restrictive and exclusionary. Will life in this planet Earth be safe and secure?

References

1. *The Challenge to the South,* Report of the South Commission, Oxford University Press, 1990.
2. *Enough is Enough,* Apex Press, 1990.
3. *GATT Agreement—Final Text,* World Trade Centre, Academy of Business Studies, 1993.
4. Sherle. R. Schwenntneer: "Reinvigorating The Global Economy", *World Policy Journal,* Summer 1992.
5. Walter Russel Mead: "The World Economic Order"—Perils After Bretton Woods" *Dissent,* Summer 1990.
6. Peter. F. Cowhey and Jonathan. D. Aronson:

   "A New Trade Order" adapted from their work *Managing the World Economy: The Consequences of Corporate Alliances,* NY; Council on Foreign Relations, Reprinted in *Foreign Affairs: America and the World,* 1992/93.

The Emerging World Order

*Prof. Ninan Koshy**

"The New Disorder" was the title of a speech made by Douglas Hurd, Foreign Secretary of Great Britain, at Chatham House, London, in January 1993. That seems to be an apt description of the world today.

For some time it was fashionable to speak of the new world order. The visionary rhetoric of a new world order is very old, used by statesmen and politicians from time to time. In the recent period the slogan came into vogue in the wake of the Gulf crisis and in the midst of the most massive military preparations in modern times.

On March 6, President Bush addressed a joint session of the US Congress and announced that "Aggression is defeated. The war is over". He was speaking about the Gulf war. It was a war which enabled the United Nations to "fulfil the historic vision of its founders. Now we can see a new world order coming into view. A world in which there is the very real prospect of a new world order. A.world in which freedom and respect for human rights find a home among all nations".[1]

While many believed that the end of the Cold War provided an unprecedented opportunity to build a new world order, linking that claim with the military success of the allied nations in the Gulf war was not reassuring.

Little is heard about the new world order now. The prevailing chaos is more aptly described as disorder.

But all agree that the Cold War has ended; the bipolar world of East and West is no more; the old international order is gone.

However, the term 'new world order is useful not because there is a new 'order' but because it provides an analytical tool to look at the previous order and the emerging trends. The persistence of old political vices is highlighted by reference to the virtue promised by a new world order. For many it is difficult to see what is new and many fear that what may be presented as new may not be better than the old. Selectivity when taking decisive action in support of international law is exposed by the universalist promise of world order. There seem to be different standards for application in the different. While actions are effectively implimented for some issues,

* Worlds Council of Churches, Geneva.

with regards to some others there is no attempt to implement decisions. There is the charge of double standards by world bodies. The prevalent disorder in so many regions contrasts neatly with the hopes of stability implied by 'order'. It is difficult to see where the order is today. It may be suggested that the phrase new world order is merely descriptive requiring no more than the acceptance that the current situation is clearly different in several respects from the one that obtained just a few years ago.

The previous order was generally described in terms of bipolarity. The global reach of both the superpowers and their tendency to interpret developments in all regions in terms of their underlying antagonism resulted in bipolarity coming to be held as the defining feature of the contemporary international system. International relations in fact meant the relations between the U.S.A and the U.S.S.R. When these improved or worsened, it was felt all over the world. It appeared that the decisions for the whole world were taken in two capitals. So long as the bipolar framework appeared to be durable, security focused on the military aspects of the equilibrium. There was good reason to believe that fear of nuclear war was an important element of stability at least in Europe. The determination, in both Washington and Moscow to prevent the logic of confrontation leading to a catastrophic conclusion, meant that the bipolar system depended on tacit co-operation and understanding as much as pure antagonism.

"The Cold War had certain rules of the game which were tacitly accepted by the two superpowers of the time. Ethically many of these rules were questionable. These rules were dependent both on ideological competition and mutual acceptance of spheres of influence. Significantly while both superpowers relied on nuclear deterrence for their security there was a taboo on the actual use of nuclear weapons, even though occasionally explicit threats were made. Nuclear deterrence is basically evil because of the continuing threat to inflict massive damage on one's enemy and the very credibility of deterrence depends on the willingness to carry out such a threat. Moreover the morality of spheres of influence was also always questionable."[2]

Bipolarity, however, did not explain all international relations and it was challenged by the non-aligned states but it was the lens through which the powerful Cold War warriors judged and perceived the world. When Britain's Prime Minister Harold Macmillain made his famous "Wind of Change" speech in South Africa in 1960, to the Africans it was a message of acceptance by him of the end of Western colonialism. But for Macmillain himself the "great issue" of the second half of the twentieth century was "whether the uncommitted peoples of Africa will swing to the East or the West. The struggle is joined and it is a struggle for the minds of men".

In 1946, Vyacheslav Molotov, the Soviet Foreign Minister, declared, "One cannot decide now any serious problems of international relations without the Soviet Union". There, in a nutshell, is the hallmark of a "superpower". With the disintegration of the Soviet Union, only the United States can now make that claim.

It was the abortive coup in Moscow in August 1991 that marked the disintegration of the Soviet Union but the Cold War had ended even before that. The dissolution of the Soviet system was the result of forces unleashed by Gorbachev's "glasnost" and "perestroika", forces which he had hoped could be controlled and directed by a reformed Communist Party. These forces gathered their own momentum and direction and led to the dramatic transformation inside Soviet Union and the whole of Eastern Europe.

The breakdown of the communist regimes in Eastern Europe has been one of the most momentous events since the end of the Second World War. It transformed East-West relations and also brought in new dimensions in North-South relations. One superpower was withdrawn from the global scene.

The unipolar model also offers only a partial explanation of the world situation. The U.S.A. remains a superpower in military terms, but it occupies a less than commanding role in international economy. A unipolar hegemony cannot be maintained in the new economic financial-technological age. The end of dominance by the two superpowers has naturally released a number of new forces and made a number of actors on the global scene more prominent.

The U.S is conscious of this and American policy is 'therefore' becoming more selective, more based on interests which can be directly related to its needs, than the comprehensive cover of the global superpower and alliance leader. Its recent policies on Europe show this. But there is still the belief about its special mission, as it were, "I am convinced that only the United States can play the leadership role that we ought to be playing, to try to stick up for the alleviation of human suffering, the continued march of democracy and human rights, and the continued growth of market economies", President Clinton has asserted. Although he spoke of a reduction in United States armed forces, he added his determination "to keep this country the strongest in the world".[3]

Integration and Disintegration

An important feature of the emerging global situation is the contest between the forces of integration and those of fragmentation. On the one hand, barriers that have historically separated nations and peoples in such areas as politics, economics, technology and culture are breaking down; especially technology and economics have become truly transnational. The advances in communication and information technology have destroyed many frontiers between nations. Inter-governmental organizations and multilateral institutions have gained new strength. On the other hand, forces of disintegration within nations and states are gathering momentum. Large states whose continued existence has been taken for granted have broken into pieces. New demands and revival of old demands for nationhood threaten many more states. Look at Europe. One can see both forces at work. While the process of integration proceeds, albeit with difficulty, it is disintegration that is prominent in the European scene as a whole. Globally also this is true and it appears that the forces of disintegration are stronger at the moment.

Ethnic Conflicts

The disorder in the international scene is to some extent caused by ethnic conflicts. Ethnicity has become possibly the predominant grass roots political unit in the world today. "The importance of ethnic conflict, as a force shaping human affairs, as a phenomenon to be understood, as a threat to be controlled, can no longer be denied. By one reckoning, ethnic violence since World War II has claimed more than ten million lives and in the last two decades ethnic conflict has become especially widespread. Ethnicity is at the centre of politics in country after country, a potent source of challenges to the cohesion of states and of international tension. Connections between Biafra, Bangladesh and Burundi, Beirut, Brussels, and Belfast were at first hesitantly made—isn't one "tribal", one "linguistic", another "religious"?—but that is true no longer. Ethnicity has fought and bled and burned its way into public and scholarly consciousness",[4] so wrote Donald L. Horovitz in 1985.

Today the consciousness is underlined by the tragic events in Bosnia, Somalia and a number of other places.

Horovitz offers an explanation, "Ethnic conflict is of course, a recurrent phenomenon. Shifting contexts make ethnicity now more, now less prominent. The international environment plays a part in its emergence and remission. Often overshadowed by international warfare and marked by wartime alliance ethnic allegiances are usually revived by the wartime experience or emerge again soon afterward, as they did after the First and Second World Wars. In their periodic re-emergence, ethnic sentiments have been supported by the widespread diffusion of the doctrine, of "national self-determination".[5]

As it happened at the end of World War I and World War II ethnicity has re-emerged with new vigour at the end of the Cold War.

Certain worldwide ideological and institutional currents have also underpinned the growth of ethnic conflict. The spread of norms of equality has made ethnic subordination illegitimate and spurred ethnic groups everywhere to compare their standing in society against that of groups in close proximity. The state system provides the framework in which ethnic conflict occurs. Control of the state, control of a state and exemption from control by other are among the main goals of ethnic conflict. Ethnic conflict today possesses elements of universality and uniformity that were not present at earlier times.

These conflicts have already challenged and in several cases redrawn the boundaries and borders that had assumed validity and even sanctity after the World War II.

As Erskine Childers points out, "Throughout the Cold War period, ancient cultural, ethnic and linguistic groups remained trapped and largely dismembered within artifical frontiers that had been imposed among them by Belgium, Britain, France, Italy, Germany, the Netherlands, Portugal and Spain, as well as Czarist and then Soviet Russia. Frontiers had been erected between people of the same culture, language and historical governance who had never known such barriers.

This giant phenomenon of peoples, cultures, and resources trapped within exogenous and economically irrational boundaries has been a devastating handicap to the stable and liberal systems of governance, and to socio-economic advancement, among most of humankind."[6]

He adds, "What is now revealed is like a vast minefield re-exposed over much of the earth's surface after decades of submergence under ice. Seventy years of imperial boundaries evaporated within weeks after the collapse of the USSR unleashing ancient ethnic and other tensions that are already exploding across European state frontiers, with tragic violence and human rights deprivations. The distinct peoples of the Central Asian Republics, only created in the 1920s by the USSR must now struggle to build comfortable politics."[7]

The redrawing of national boundaries, a process which apparently has not stopped, has made the *distinction* between internal and international conflicts even more difficult. Internal conflicts used to become *internationalized* as a result of intervention by outside *states directly or indirectly. But when multinational states* break up and new nations are only in the process of being recognized by the international community there is a real difficulty in distinguishing between internal and international conflicts. From the time the United Nations adopted the first resolution on Yugoslavia in September, 1991 till it expelled Yugoslavia from the United Nations a year later, the world body acted on the assumption it was dealing with an internal conflict whereas the fact of the matter was that the old Yugoslavia had already ceased to exist by June, 1991. The UN's difficulty was understandable especially because in terms of any intervention by the United Nations the distinction between internal and international conflict was crucial and decisive.

Politics and Religion

A prominent feature on the international scene is the apparent growing influence of religion in the politics of identity, ethnic and nationalistic. There are situations where ethnicity or nationalism is coterminous with a religion or a denomination of a religion. So when references are made to Armenians they are Christians and Azerbaijanis are Muslims. In former Yugoslavia where genocide is given respectability by calling it ethnic cleansing it is conveniently forgotten that the Muslims of Bosnia are also Serbs. This identification of nationalism with religion poses a challenge to secular polity in many states. "The new world order that is replacing the bipolar power of the old cold war is characterized not only by the rise of new economic forces, a crumbling of old empires and the discrediting of communism, but also by the resurgence of parochial identities based on ethnic and religious identities".[8] Some argue that this has happened because of the failure of secular nationalism. The Western models of nationhood—both democratic and socialist—are seen to have failed and religion is seen as a hopeful alternative, a base for criticism and change.

Some others interpret it in a slightly different way. "As political ideology recedes with the collapse of communism, the politics of identity and community of religion, ethnicity and gender have begun to occupy the space vacated by political ideology. Directly and indirectly, religion, ethnicity and gender increasingly define what politics is about, from the standing of Muslim personal law and monuments in India to Muslim and Christian Serbs and Croats sharing sovereignty in Bosnia to the Clinton Administration's effort to appoint a government that "looks like America".[9]

It is not only secular nationalism that is under threat but also pluralist political systems and societies. This has also resulted in insecurity and frustration of minorities and denial of their democratic rights.

It is the influence of political Islam that is often cited as the evidence of threatening religious revival with political consequences. The assumption that there is genuine religious renaissance and consequent political organization is not valid. It is true that there is political mobilization in many countries misusing religion and religious identity. But this is not confined to Islamic countries.

One hears often about Islamic threat. Islamic fundamentalism is pictured as the new enemy. It is true that Islam today constitutes the most pervasive and powerful transnational force in the world. "For a western World long accustomed to a global vision and foreign policy predicated upon superpower rivalry for global influence if not dominace—it is all too tempting to identify another global, ideological menace to fill the threat vacuum created by the demise of communism".[10] However, it is political myopia that views that Muslim world and the Islamic movements as a monolith and seeing them solely in terms of extremism and terrorism. While violent actions of the few are generalized the legitimate aspirations and policies of the many are not properly understood. A selective presentation and analysis of Islam and of events in the Muslim World have led to conclusions which are misleading and often alarmist.

Western secular presuppositions have been a major obstacle in understanding Islamic politics and so have contributed to a tendency to reduce Islam to fundamentalism and fundamentalism to religious extremism. The many forces of contemporary Islamic revivalism tended to be subsumed under the monolith of "Islamic fundamentalism" which was equated with violence and fanaticism with mullah-led theocracies or small radical guerilla groups.

The Nation-State

In the post-Cold War period several questions have been raised about the future of the nation-state. Their role has been challenged by other actors on the scene. New notions about sovereignty, legitimacy and international recognition have affected the quality of states. Demographic, economic, environmental and technological changes, all transnational in nature, have serious implications for the future of the nation-state itself.

But the continued prominence of the governments of states as the major shapers of internation structures has to be readily conceded. "They are not the only international actors; they differ substantially in size and strength; many have very limited capacity; some are unstable and other have even disintegrated; each has to modify its behaviour according to circumstances and the reactions of other international actors (government and non-government), and states often fail to address adequately issues which are of great importance for the world's future such as the environment. Yet for all their limitations they are the main building blocks of international structures."[11]

Paul Kennedy asks the question, "Are not the important actors in world affairs now-a-days the global corporations? Isn't technology creating winners and losers—in employment and career patterns—regardless of where one lives? In an age of twentyfour-hour-a-day currency trading or for that matter global warning have national bodies such as cabinets or commerce departments much relevance?"[12]

The global changes also call into question the usefulness of the nation-state itself. The key autonomous actor in political and international affairs for the past few centuries appears not just to be losing its control and integrity but to be the wrong sort of unit to handle the newer circumstances. "For some problems, it is too large to operate effectively; for others,it is too small. In consequence, there are pressures for a "relocation of authority" both upward and downward, creating structures that might respond better to today's and tomorrow's forces for change".[13]

Kenechi Ohmae further says, "The nation-state has become an unnatural even dysfunctional unit for organising human activity and managing economic endeavour in a borderless world. It represents no genuine shared community of economic interests. It defines no meaningful flows of economic activity. In fact, it overlooks the true linkages and synergies that exist among often disparate populations by combining important measure of human activity at the wrong level of analysis."[14]

The "relocation of authority" of which Paul Kennedy speaks is in some ways related to the new discussion on sovereignty.

The former Secretary-General of the United Nations, in his last report to the General Assembly, took up this issue from the point of view of human rights. "The case for not impinging on the sovereignty, territorial integrity and political independence of states is by itself indubitably strong. But it would only be weakened if it were to carry the implication that sovereignty, even in this day and age includes the right of mass slaughter or of launching systematic campaigns of decimation or forced exodus of civilian populations in the name of controlling civil strike or insurrection."[15]

The South

Another feature of the new global situation is the enormous weakening of the South. A number of factors have contributed to this. The end of the Cold War has meant that the strategy of many third world countries to play one superpower against the other is no longer effective. It is also true that for several reasons the Soviet Union and its allies championed many Third World causes and in international fora used their strength to espouse and garner support for them. Such support is no longer there.

Today third world countries have become more and more dependent on the West and on institutions controlled by them like the World Bank and the International Monetary Fund. Globalisation has considerably affected their domestic economic policies which are increasingly decided outside. The economic dependence has reduced their political manoeuvrability in the international arena at a time when the Cold War's end challenges the raison d'etre of nonalignment.

The Non-Aligned Movement manages to give the impression that it still continues. This is possible only because it refrains from taking clear positions on a number of issues on which a movement like it should uphold its principles. The movement originated as an attempt to steer clear of the two power blocs but its policies often found much in common with the position of the Soviet Union. It often took an anti-Western stance and with full justification. Today it finds itself in a situation of not being able to criticise the West, especially the USA, with the increasing economic and military dependence of most of its constituents on the USA, though in fact there are a number of issues on which the U.S deserves criticism.

The North-South relations in the coming decade will be of crucial significance in international relations. The South has not been able to articulate a coherent position in the post-Cold War period while the North is keen to absorb parts of the Third World in its economy and leave the rest of it to its desperation. The South seems to have lost not only its voice but the vocabulary.

Human Rights Today

The increasing acceptance of the universality of human rights and the international community's responsibility for human rights everywhere is a welcome feature of the emerging international scene.

Universality is inherent in human rights. As the Secretary, General of the UN told the World Human Rights Conference "The Charter is categorical on this score; Article 55 states that the United Nations shall promote "Universal respect for and observance of, human rights and fundamental freedoms for all without distinction as to race, sex, language or religion. "The title of the 1948 Declaration - universal, not international-reinforces this perspective."[16]

However the conference itself showed that universality is accepted with reservations by several countries which define human rights in religious, cultural, economic and social terms. The Secretary-General of the UN admitted, "While human rights represent a common objective for the members of the international community as a whole, while each member of that community recognizes itself in that issue, each culture has its own special way of framing the question".[17]

There are observers who feel that ironically the end of the Cold War and the apparent consensus between the East and the West might have undermined important dimensions in the discourse on international human rights. The three generations of human rights broadly corresponded to three political visions. Generally civil and political rights were associated with Western Liberal Democracies, social and economic rights with East European socialist states and development rights with post-colonial developing countries.

In spite of the attempt to be comprehensive the Vienna Declaration gives disproportionate prominence to the concept of civil and political rights and does not reflect adequately the evolution of human rights through the United Nations in the eighties.

Perhaps more significant is the widening of differences between the North and the South in spite of the compromises at Vienna. The views of the South were already clearly expressed at the meeting of the Heads of State and Governments of the Security Council in January, 1982. The Chinese Prime Minister, while conceding that "human rights and fundamental freedoms of mankind should be universally respected", stated that "the issue of human rights fell within the sovereignty of each country and should not be judged in disregard of its history and national conditions. It was neither appropriate nor workable to demand that all countries measure up to the human rights criteria or model of one or a small number of countries".[18] The Indian Prime Minister took up the same argument and said that "it was important to note that the content and nature of human rights were conditioned by the social, traditional and cultural forces that prevailed in different societies. While the endeavour of the UN was to gradually move towards creating uniform international norms for human rights, such norms should not be unilaterally defined and set up as absolute preconditions for interatction between societies in the political or economic spheres.[19]

These arguments were repeated again before and at the Vienna Conference.

The United Nations

It is the transformation in the position and profile of the United Nations which is perhaps the most remarkable feature in the global scene. There is a renewed sense of energy. Expectations and hopes about the UN have never been so high. Whether the UN will be able to sustain and fulfil them is the big question. The Secretary-General has warned against an "excess of credibility". He did so because he was conscious of the UN's vulnerability as well as its opportunity.

With the end of the long years of Cold War deadlock on security issues, the Security Council, operating closer to the intention of the Charter than at any time in history, has been active in a number of trouble spots.

The UN Charter lays down the principles and structure of the organization. It reflects the fact that the UN is not a world government but an arena of sovereign states. There is an in-built tension between the Charter's respect for universal and individual rights and the claims of its member-states.

Demands are growing for the reform of the United Nations. One of the usual and more pressing demands is for the restructuring of the Security Council. The present permanent membership of the Security Council reflects the power equation at the end of the Second World War. As the "Economist" observed:"The Security Council is absurdly anachronistic" and even reasonable reforms "would be vetoed by France and Britain, sticking limpetlike to their nuclear-armed chairs". Many of the UN's 183 members felt alienated by the Council, which since the end of the Cold War, has been dominated by the western three (Russia has been preoccupied with domestic matters; China is not greatly concerned with faraway places). The Security Council, say its harshest critics, has become little more than an extra arm of western foreign policy".[20]

In its statement of 31 January 1992, adopted at the conclusion of the first meeting held by the Security Council at the level of Heads of State and government, the Secretary-General was instructed to prepare an "analysis and recommendations on ways of strengthening and making more efficient within the framework and provisions of the Charter the capacity of the United Nations for preventive diplomacy, for peacemaking and for peacekeeping". The Report given by the Secretary-General has two important new aspects. One is the concept of peace-building action to identify and support structures which will tend to strengthen and solidify peace in order to avoid a relapse into conflict.

The second and more important was the proposal to have under the Security Council armed forces on a permanent basis to be deployed for the maintenance or restoration of international peace and security. The Security Council has so far not acted on this proposal.

In the recent past the United Nations has taken action in a number of situations which might be described as internal conflicts of memeber countries. Actions with regard to Northern Iraq, former Yugoslavia, Somalia, Cambodia etc. though of different character have raised a number of critical questions with regard to the international community's role in internal conflicts.

Fred Halliday in a recent article points out that there are three kinds of responses to the emerging global situation. "One is an optimistic one, that sees the world as having moved decisively forward and as being in a period when certain desirable goals—peace, democracy and greater prosperity—are now available to all. The second is a pessimism of the left which asserts that we are in a new imperialist epoch—that the North is incapable of assisting in the development of the South, that ecological destruction is oncoming, that the USA will, on its own, or in association with its old allies, use the new opportunities to dominate the world. An alternative form of pessimism, a gloomy sobriety of the Right, sees the breakdown of the Cold War as, in many respects, a return to the world before 1914, or between the two World Wars leading to greater inter-state conflict, nuclear proliferation and hyper-nationalism.

Halliday says, "These approaches have the merit of making sense of the world, but in some obvious respects they are all deficient".[21]

"An agenda for dealing with this new world involves at least four different issues. In the first place, it requires a balanced assessment of the situation of power in the contemporary world, and of the possibilities open to those states with the greatest amount of it.

Secondly, it requires a recognition within the richer and more powerful countries that in the post-Cold War world a retreat to a narrow definition of 'national interest' is both impossible and morally reprehensible...

Thirdly at the political-strategic level the question is how far a system of peaceful and cooperative relations between states can be maintained in a post-Cold War world.

Fourthly, beyond these political issues, there is the question of how the evident universalising trends in the world political and economic system will prevail in diffusing prosperity and in reducing the gap between rich and poorer states".[22]

References

1. New York Times, 7 March 1991.
2. Stanley Hoffman, "Ethics and the Rules of the Game between the Superpowers", Right vs Might (Council on Foreign Relations, New York), 1989, p.84.
3. Anthony Hartley, "The Clinton Approach: Idealism with Prudence", "The Wolrd Today", London, February, 1993.
4. Donald L. Horowitz, "Ethnic Groups in Conflict", University of California Press, Berkeley, 1985, p.xi.
5. Ibid., p.4
6. Erskine Childers,"UN Mechanisms and Capacities for Interventions" "in "The challenge to Intervene. A New Role for the United Nations". Ed. Elizabeth Ferris, Life and Peace Institute, Uppsals, 1992, p.11.
7. Ibid., p.43.
8. Mark Juergensmeyer, "The New Cold War". University of California Press, Berkeley, 1993, p.l.
9. Susanne Hoeber Rudolph and Lloyd I. Rudolph "Modern Hatred". The New Republic, March 22, 1993, p.29.
10. John L. Esposito, "The islamic Threat", Oxford University Press, Oxford, 1992, p.4.
11. James Barbar, "The Search for International Order and Justice". "The World Today". August-September, 1993, p.156.
12. Paul Kennedy, "Preparing for the Twenty-first Century", Harper Collins, London, 1993, pp. 122-123.
13. Ibid., p.131.
14. Kenechi Ohmae, "The Rise of the Region State", "Foreign Affairs, Spring 1993, p.78.
15. U.N., Docs, GA/46/1 p.10
16. U.N., Press Release SC/SM/5012, 14 June, 1993.
17. Ibid.,

18. U.N. Docs, SC/5359, 31 January, 1992.
19. Ibid.
20 "The Economist," London, 12 June, 1993, p.22.
21. Fred Halliday, "Balance Sheet of 1993: The New World and its Discontents" Mainstream, January 8, 1994, p.10.
22. Ibid p.13-14.

4

The Emerging World System : Advantages and Disadvantages for the United States

*Tom A. Travis**

In recent years, the political structure of the international system has dramatically shifted from bipolarity to unipolarity, and the Cold War has ended. Less change has occurred in the international economy, although the capitalist world system has now penetrated every corner of the globe, and countries world-wide are rushing to privatise their economies. As changes occur in the international system, the distribution of global wealth, power, status, and benefit is altered. These changes, in turn, contribute to the reshaping of national foreign policies.

The purposes of this essay are to discuss the main features of the emerging international system and the effects on U.S. foreign policy. First, the salient characteristics of the world system likely to exist into the early twenty-first century will be sketched. Second, the specific advantages and disadvantages for the United States in this international system will be analyzed. Last, conclusions will be reached about the extent to which the United States will benefit or lose from the emerging world system and about the implications for the future global order.

The Main Features of the Emerging International System

The main characteristics of the international system likely to exist into the early twenty-first century are described below.

* Political Science Department, Bucknell University, Lewisburg, Pennsylvania, US

Values

In the value dimension, liberalism (democratic capitalism) has superseded socialism (socialist dictatorship) and will continue to be incorporated in one form or another into Eastern Europe, Russia, some of the former Soviet republics and into a growing number of third world countries, including former marxist states like China and Vietnam. Capitalism is more likely to be successfully introduced than democracy in many of these nations.

Western, particularly American values and attitudes of individualism, materialism, consumption, and self-gratification in an urban, industrial, high technology context will continue to be rapidly spread across the world by American and European media and transnational corporations. To some extent, there has been a return culturally to the nineteenth century in terms of the global scope and influence of liberalism, at least among the elite classes of most countries.

Socialism has been replaced by religious fundamentalism, particularly in its Islamic form, as the main counter-ideology. For the time being, this movement will be a minor global competitor to liberalism. However, if liberalism should prove to be individually unsatisfying or unsuccessful in spurring rapid development, then anti-liberal ideologies, whether socialistic, fascistic, or religious fundamentalist, could gain greater appeal and become major threats to liberalism in the early twenty-first century.

Objectives

The dominant objectives for the foreseeable future will be those of the G-7 powers and their financial institutions and will largely emphasize the status quo—global capitalism, Euro-North American international law and rules, global "free" trade, and inequality in wealth, power, and status.

There is little new about these goals. What is different is that the number of states advocating revolutionary goals has substantially shrunk, given the disappearance of the Soviet Union and Eastern bloc and the moderation of former revisionist states like China, Syria, Vietnam, and Cuba. For the next decade, the main opposition to the G-7 objectives will not be revolutionary, but reformist, emanating from some Third World governments which seek modification of global rules to create a less unequal world. In the following decade, if a greater number of states adopt anti-liberal ideologies and become deeply resentful about inequalities of global wealth and power, a revolutionary challenge to G-7 objectives could reappear.

Power

The bipolar system has been replaced by a unipolar oligarchical, concert system of the G-7, led on most dimensions by the United States. Power is reminiscent of the nineteenth century concert system (expanded to include North America and Japan), although the United States does not hold full hegemonic power as Great Britain did at that time. While Washington will exert disproportionate influence on most issues, it will have to consult with its G-7 allies and sometimes make concessions, as it has on Bosnia and trade. Led by the United States, more often than not, the G-7 powers will act in concert to manage the world system in ways consistent with their ideological preferences and pragmatic interests.

There will be no other country or coalition capable of matching the power of the G-7. The main past challenger, the Soviet bloc, has disappeared. Russia will remain too pre-occupied with internal problems and too reliant on G-7 support for its liberal experiment to exert independent power on most issues.

Certain non-state actors, including TNCs, TNBs, the U.N. Security Council and U.N. financial institutions will experience some increase in power, but will largely operate within the confines of G-7 guidance and control.

Most Third World governments will have less global power in the unipolar system than in the past. They have lost sources of influence they possessed in the bipolar period. They can no longer practise non-alignment in terms of manoeuvering between the blocs to gain diplomatic latitude. In the post bipolar world, most developing countries have become less geo-strategically important. As a result, they will have less opportunity to link strategically to a major power in exchange for reciprocal benefit. Southern states may be able to exert negative influence, resisting the demands of the G-7 powers. However, they will run the risk of incurring G-7 sanctions, as has happened recently to Libya and Haiti. Third World governments will rarely be able to exercise positive power to implement their preferred agendas against the wishes of the G-7. The G-7 will probably be more tolerant of increased regional power of key Southern governments, as long as the main interests of the Northern powers are not jeopardized.

China is the developing country with the highest global power potential, but it is likely to remain a "sleeping giant" for at least the next decade or two. Its global aims remain modest and it has shown little inclination to project itself a major world power or to challenge the G-7 governments on most critical issues.

The United States has become the single military superpower in terms of capability. When Washington chooses to exert military leadership, it will usually be able to mobilize a coalition to employ military force as it did in the Persian Gulf. There no longer is a credible military balancer against the United States and its alliances, which will allow them to use force largely as they wish against non-nuclear states. The U.N. Security Council has renewed its collective security role and has expanded its peace-keeping activities. However, it will continue to operate mainly as an instrument of the G-7 powers which will preclude any inependent authority.

The International Economy

The economic dimension will remain hierarchical with power concentrated in the G-7 and its associated financial non-state institutions. The United States has increasingly had to share its power with Germany, the European Community, Japan, and large transnational firms, and this trend will continue. These actors, reaching common decisions through competitive bargaining, will jointly manage the world capitalist economy. If the recent GATT agreement unravels and economic conflict intensifies between the United States, Japan, and the European Union, trading blocs centered around these actors could emerge. Even in this case, there would be sufficient cooperation among the leaders of the trading blocs to supervise the world economy.

The international capitalist system, more widespread and powerful than ever before, will operate—as it always has—to disproportionately benefit the core states and their financial institutions at the expense of the vast majority of citizens of the peripheral states situated mainly in the Third World.

With exceptions, Southern states have been losing economic power relative to Northern states and will become increasingly marginalized and dependent. They will have little say in economic decisions that will affect them, and will be under great pressure to comply to the trade, investment and intellectual property regimes that the G-7 establishes to guide the world economy.

International Rules

The rules of behaviour, manifested in international law and custom, will remain almost entirely Northern- centric and serve the interests of the OECD states and their associated financial institutions, as they have for centuries. The number of authoritative regimes on the environment, telecommunications, trade, investment, intellectual property and weapons non-proliferation will grow. However, these regimes will continue to be shaped largely by the needs of the G-7 states and will be monitored carefully by these powers to ensure that their interests are preserved.

With the disappearance of the Soviet bloc, which followed somewhat different rules within its coalition and was attempting to revise the global norms, the Northern rules have become fully global. The monopoly of power of the G-7 coalition will enable it to enforce these rules thoroughly, again reminiscent of the nineteenth century. The G-7 states are assertively demanding that their preferred rules on weapons non-proliferation, human rights, intellectual property, and economic liberalization be followed and expect their calls to be heeded. Any revisionist or revolutionary states that emerge in the future will try to challenge these rules, but will lack the power to change them.

Positive and Negative Effects of the Emerging World Order

The effects of these features of the "new" world order will be diverse. The effects cannot be discussed in detail here. Only the main security and economic implications will be briefly presented.

Warfare

The elimination of bipolarity, a major source of warfare of the past half century, coupled with unipolar military power and a more credible threat of U.N. Security Council collective security action, should diminish (but not end) inter-state warfare. Such warfare will mainly be between third world states and among former Soviet republics over territorial and irridentist issues.

If the result of armed force should be the elimination of the sovereignty of a long-term state (Kuwait but not Bosnia or Georgia), U.N. Security Council intervention, spearheaded by the United States, will be probable, a deterrent in itself. After the Persian Gulf, would-be aggressors, other than nuclear powers with global reach, will have to be cautious about their military ventures.

The United States has great military capability. However, bipolarity, the main source of past U.S. military intervention has ended; the United States has learned from bitter experience about the difficulty of using force in civil conflicts; the U.S goverment is pre-occupied with domestic concerns, and Congress and the public oppose an active American military role. As a result, it is likely that Washington will lack the will and commitment to frequently use force as a foreign policy instrument. The United States will find that diplomatic and economic sanctions will usually be sufficient to get its way. What force Washington does use will typically result from consultation with its G-7 partners and be coordinated with its military allies or the U.N. Security Council.

The rise of ethnic and religious nationalism, socio-economic inequality and illegitimate governments will increase intra-state civil, secessionist and revolutionary wars, particularly in the Third World and Eurasia. Internal conflict will become the primary form of warfare. In the absence of bipolarity, domestic wars are more likely to remain free from great power intervention and to be contained locally.

It is also probable that the U.N. Security Council will become more selective about its peace-keeping intervention in intrernal wars, given the difficulty of ending such conflicts and of raising sufficient finances and troops. If the U.N. campaign in Somalia should fail and the civil war in Cambodia should resume, then it will be difficult to sustain enthusiasm for peace-keeping in the future.

Particularly in the North, military spending will decline and military industrial complexes will be down-sized. However, despite G-7 efforts to strengthen weapon non-proliferation regimes, advanced weapons will continue to spread which will make warfare, domestic and international, increasingly bloody. The victims will mainly be citizens of Eurasia and the Third World. It is unlikely, for at least the next two decades, that third world states possessing advanced weapons would target the Northern powers and risk devastating retaliation.

International Economy

With the decline of inter-state warfare, the economic dimension of international relations will become ever more important. Economic issues will be addressed in frequent conferences, particularly among the G-7 and OECD actors, in an effort to shape and enforce global economic regimes that serve their interests.

Whatever economic interdependence, integration and benefit occur, will largely be confined to the OECD states, especially the G-7 and, to a set of semi- peripheral states in the South, including the oil rich, low population states of West Asia, the Asian NICs, and China. The majority of third world states will be more marginalized, dependent and disadvantaged in the "new" world order than in the old.

This inequality is built into the nature of the world capitalist system whose institutions, regimes and rules serve the interests of the core states more than the periphery. For the next decade at least, the more developed countries, many of which are financially strapped and face domestic problems, will be unlikely to offer international economic reforms, such as an NIEO, or to act generously to ease the plight of the least developed countries. Many of the trends of the international economy that have been unfavourable to most third world states, including falling raw material commodity prices, mounting debt, and rising capital outflow, will continue. Also, the international system will intensify some of the impediments to development that lie within many developing countries, such as corruption, wasteful spending and ecological decay. As a result, the economic prognosis for the majority of Southern states, particularly in Africa and Latin America is dim. The economic prospects for China, the Asian NICs, and the petroleum states of West Asia are better.

In sum, the world will consist of a small number of privileged, powerful states, largely those of the OECD, favoured by peace, prosperity, and some ecological quality, and a much larger number of marginalized states in the Third World plagued by warfare, civil unrest, unstable government, economic stagnancy, and environmental decay. Some states, of course, will be in between.

Effects of the Emerging International System on U.S. Foreign Policy

The discussion so far suggests that the United States will be advantaged in the emerging world order. Generally, that is true, and should come as no surprise. However, more specifically, there are new advantages and disadvantages for the United States that need to be examined.

Advantages for the United States

The United States will profit substantially from the post bipolar system. The United States is more secure now than in the past half century without the threat of the Soviet Union or any other well armed challenger and without much danger of nuclear warfare. As a result, Washington will have the opportunity to reduce its military industrial complex and military budget, as well as its military commitments and use of force abroad.

Without a global balancer against the United States, Washington will be able to use force when necessary against non-nuclear states without fear of devastating retaliation. It will usually be able to count on the U.N. Security Council to legitimize its military ventures and on greater burden sharing from allies in multi-lateral actions, as in the Persian Gulf and Somalia.

As the United States reduces its military expenditures and foreign deployments, it will be able to concentrate, instead, on retooling its domestic economy, shrinking its budget deficit, and mitigating its domestic ills, all essential to improving its competitive position in the world economy.

While the United States has less relative economic power in the 1990s than in the past, it still remains the most powerful world economy in many dimensions. As the new GATT agreement is implemented, Washington should be able to pry open the markets of other countries in ways favourable to American business and should benefit to some degree from an expanded and "free" global market economy.

The United States has a unique opportunity to remake Russia and former Soviet bloc countries in its own image, as it did with Germany and Japan after World War II. If Washington succeeds, it will be able to turn these states into long-term allies, short-run dependents, and favourable market and investment outlets, as well as improve the prospects for world peace.

The United States will have heightened influence over third world governments for reasons already discussed. In the unipolar world, it is important for developing countries to appease Washington and seek its goodwill. The United States can use its improved power position to press Southern governments to accept its expanding agenda on human rights, nuclear non-proliferation, advanced weapons technology controls, intellectual property, economic liberalization, and the like. Former Third World revisionists, like Syria, Libya, Vietnam and Cuba, must be more circumspect and moderate in their foreign policies in order to avoid US/G-7 sanctions. This moderation will ease the American task of managing the world order.

Without the bipolar system and America's past anti-communist phobia, the United States should be able to adopt a more flexible, complex foreign policy to better take advantage of new international opportunities. Its foreign policy process may also become more open and democratic which could restrain officials from some of the excesses of the past.

Disadvantages for the United States

There are also new costs and dangers for the United States. U.S. security could be short-lived if the liberal experiment in Russia should fail and the socialist system or Cold War reappear. Fortunately, for the United States, the latter two outcomes are unlikely. On the other hand, there is high potential for civil conflict throughout Eurasia and for inter-state warfare among the former Soviet republics. As these conflicts mount, the calls for American or NATO military involvement in this region could rise.

Indeed, since the United States is the sole military superpower, there will be heavy world-wide demands on Washington to provide military aid and armed support to beleaguered countries. Whether the United States acts unilaterally, through NATO or the United Nations, it will have to make difficult choices about when and where to render such aid.

If the United States plays an extensive role as global police official, it could get enmeshed in interminable, costly conflicts with high human and financial costs. The United States, then, would be unable to substantially curb its military expenditures which would harm its economy and exacerbate domestic ailments. On the other hand, if Washington too often declines to exert military leadership, it could be seen as a paper tiger, deficient in courage, commitment and will. This reputation would diminish its superpower status.

The latter reputation would have far-reaching effects. The military pillar of the unipolar system would erode and interstate warfare could increase. Potential aggressors might take heart and initiate military attacks, doubting the American will to resist. The nuclear non-proliferation regime so dear to Washington could unravel, as governments scramble to acquire nuclear capability to deter aggressive neighbours. American allies might feel a need to create their own nuclear arsenals to counter regional threats. If Germany and Japan should move in this direction, a multipolar system would evolve, inimical to American interests.

The life of a military superpower may be enviable, but is not without travail. It will not be easy for the U.S. government to determine its military priorities or to balance the competing demands from bureaucratic units, Congress, interest groups, the United Nations, and governments in favour or against U.S. military action.

The United States will also be faced with another dilemma. Military force will become less relevant in the post bipolar system where main international concerns will be economic, social and environmental in nature. The full array of American military power cannot solve the problems of debt, refugees, narcotics, climate change, or AIDS.

As these issues occupy more of the global agenda, it will become increasingly difficult for Washington to exercise independent power. To confront these problems, the United States will have to consult and bargain more with its G-7 partners, transnational firms, the United Nations, and NGOs. Washington has discovered that its military power is often not fungible and cannot easily be translated into influence on non-security dimensions. Furthermore, if G-7 governments like Japan and Germany should feel less need for US military protection in the post bipolar world, Washington would lose an important source of influence over them.

Despite these difficulties, the United States will still be the foremost power through the end of the century. It will strive to exert global leadership to vigorously promote its preferred world order. Once again, however, this leadership role will be a double edged sword. Some American proposals and demands will meet resistance from governments which oppose the perceived costs and do not like being told what to do. Recent examples have been the tensions between the United States and the Chinese or Indian governments over human rights, advanced weapon exports, trade, and Kashmir. In the unipolar system, the United States may be bound to lead, but this role will have costs as well as benefits.

While the Clinton administration believes the United States will gain from NAFTA and a global free trade regime, there are American economic experts who disagree. If they are correct and the United States should become flooded by inexpensive Third World imports or lose businesses and jobs to developing countries, Americans could rue the day these free trade accords were signed.

Finally, the more complex global agenda could confuse American foreign policy officials who have been used to acting in a dichotomous bipolar world where national security was the main concern. There are bound to be struggles among foreign policy officials and bureaucracies for control of US policy in the post bipolar world, and organizational routines from the Cold War period may obstruct needed policy change. These factors could undermine rational decision-making and produce foreign policy ambiguity and inconsistency, hampering Washington's ability to take full advantage of new opportunities in the emerging world order.

Conclusion

On balance, the United States should accrue greater benefit than loss from the late twentieth century world system. Some of the disadvantages can be minimized if Washington is able to correctly choose among difficult priorities and to skilfully practise diplomacy. However, it will not be easy to conduct foreign policy as the world's leading power and there will be potential for error. If the United States errs too often, and permits a trade war to occur with Japan or the European Union, fails to exert political leadership, or refuses to use its military power to quell international security threats, then global power will defuse and the unipolar system will shift toward multipolarity. A multipolar system would probably be more conflictful and dangerous than a unipolar world, but there might be greater opportunity for global justice to occur.

5

Global Economic Integration : Differential Impact Ignored

*Dr. M. Kunhaman**

The process of global integration that is currently under way has already been recognised by all. Thanks to the rapid strides made in the field of transport and communications, the world is supposed to be 'shrinking' fast. The process is sought to be encapsulated in usages such as "global village", the "global supermarket" and "global economy". While conceding the symbolic significance of these usages, it must none-the-less, be admitted that each of these is only a figure of speech and not an analytical category facilitating our understanding of a process and the implications thereof.

The bitter experiences gained from the two World Wars had ·ompted some perceptive persons to think in terms of humanity as a collectivity governed by a world government. According to this thinking, mounting world tension requires as countervailing forces, the emergence of the world citizen, establishment of an international court of justice, and the creation and maintenance of an international army. Also demanded is the establishment of an economic security council in the UN. However, the irony is that even as these world perspectives have been becoming increasingly popular, the concept of nation states has been becoming ossified making national boundaries and national sovereignty ever more sacrosanct and thereby rendering the world perspectives mere abstractions.

The *de jure* strengthening of the nation states that has been the growing tendency of the post-World War II period has, however, been progressively eroded by the operations of the multinational

* Reader Dept. of Economics, University of Kerala.

corporations, functioning with the overt as well as covert support and involvement of the ruling class of every country. In fact, when we speak about global economic integration, we are alluding to the globalisation of the market whose instrumentalities are the multinational corporations. Thus, the present globalisation is characterised by economic forces transcending political boundaries reducing, in the process, the sovereignty of nations, especially of the backward nations to mere formalities.

Facilitating the globalisation process has been the radical shift in ideology. There is no longer any talk about 'equitable growth', 'social equity' or 'socialism'. All these have become outmoded and even discredited terms. Their place has been taken over by the free market ideology— an ideology which finds its greatest appeal in the East European countries after the eclipse of socialism. The most eloquent testimony of this ideology underpinning the new economic thinking is found, without doubt, in the World Development Report 1991 whose centrepiece is "market- friendly approach". Considering the overwhelming influence of the Word Development Reports on economic thinking and policy formulation all over the world, the sweeping nature of this ideology, especially in the context of the declining importance of the socialist ideology, can be easily recognised.

Of course, the decline and fall of the socialist system and the disintegration of the former Soviet Union formed the immediate background of the global market integration.

A very important event worthy of note in conjunction with the disappearance of the socialist system is the rise of Japan as a dominant economic power. What is of great, importance in the immediate context is not Japan's position as a world political power but as a regional economic power in the Asia-Pacific region. In the fields of direct investment, exports and technology, it has pushed America to the second position as far as the region is concerned. The situation is evident from the following table:-

Positions of Japan and America in the Asia-Pacific Regions in the Case of Selected Indicator (as of 1989)

	Japan	*USA*
1. Direct Investment (in billion dollars)	$41.5	$32.0
2. Exports (in billion dollars)	$92.4	$67.9
3. Imports (in billion dollars)	$70.3	$101.3

Source: Indian Express, August 4, 1992.

According to the same source, the value of Japan's high tech exports to the region is twice that of America. In fact, the developing countries in general and those of Asia in particular regard Japan as a model, for Japan's is considered to be a story of success through disciplined and consistent hardwork. By other parameters also, Japan is ahead of America. Thus, while the proportion of disposable income saved in Japan is 15.7%, it is only 4.6% in the USA; Japan invests 35.6% of its GDP while in America, the figure is less than half at 17%. Japan's phenomenal success is attributed, *inter-alia,* to the relatively lower degree of inequality in income distribution. "America's top business executives allot themselves 119 times the pay of an ordinary worker. In Japan, the difference is only 18 times."

While recognising the increasing importance of Japan as a regional economic power, America's position of pre-eminence in the international polity and economy should not go unrecognised. It is true that America is facing many problems domestically such as budget and external deficits, internal as well as external debt, unemployment and increasing inequality.

Similarly, the racial problem, in its innumerable manifestations and ramifications, seems to tear the social fabric of the country as under. Novertheless, it is incontrovertible that America's capacity to influence the global economy and polity is ever on the increase. In this sense, as far as the global economic processes are concerned, the domestic situation in America is less important than the control it exercises over the economies of the other countries both bilaterally and through the intermediation of the multilateral financial and development agencies.

In addition to the control exercised through the multilateral institutions and agencies, the US is also able to dictate terms to the developing countries bilaterally through the use of provisions such as Super 301 and Special 301 of the US Trade Law. Likewise, even as the United States keeps advocating free trade, it is encouraging regional trade groupings. Under its initiative has been formed the NAFTA, the largest free trade bloc in the world.

Another process which will have overwhelming and far-reaching consequences is the European unification with a common currency, common foreign policy and common defence. Once the Maastricht Treaty is fully operationalized a federation of Europe is most likely to become a reality by the year 1999.

Taking cue from the behaviour of the developed countries, the developing countries are also strengthening the solidarity among themselves as is evidenced by the increasing tendency among them to take common stance on many issues at the UN. At the Earth Summit at Rio de Janeiro, they were able to present a united stand on development and environment, emphasising that the environmental problems cannot be considered in isolation from the structure of development pursued so far. Poverty, according to a few well articulate across the world, is the greatest environmental problem and therefore, in this sense, world poverty has been considered as the inevitable outcome of the structure of development which has been highly iniquitous in addition to being destructive of environment.

It is true that the developing countries did not succeed in wresting any immediate concessions from the developed countries. However, they were undoubtedly able to bring into sharper focus for the first time their basic problems which they succeeded in highlighting as the creation of the developed countries.

Alongwith the above developments , a latest phenomenon is the emergence of the possibility of a Pan Asian identity. It has increasingly been recognised that a combine of India, Japan and China can become a dynamic force in the global economic order. The recognition of this fact has, indeed, been based on incontrovertible facts. Asia is the fastest growing region in the world today. Japan is a world economic power. India and China with enormous endowments of natural resources and accounting for more than 40 percent of the world population form promising potential markets. It may be mentiond in this context that the world economic powers are evincing keen interest in the structural adjustment programmes presently underway in India and China not because these two countries are poor but because they are rich potentially as well as actually. Nobody gains from alliances with weaklings especially in the economic field.

Notwithstanding the increasing solidarity among the developing countries, some of the vulnerable spots in their existence should be noted. Of such spots, three seem to be immediately relevant: (1) The changes in the East European countries; (2) Debt crisis; and (3) Increasing differentiation of the developing countries.

The recent changes in the former Soviet Union and East European countries have not only created an ideologically unipolar world but also have tended to facilitate the global economic integration. A strong belief is being created that the world has no alternative to creating a market-based economic order. It is as if all other system have failed. However, our intentioin in the present context is not to compare the relative merits and defects of the various systems and establish the superiority of one over the others. What interests us here is that the admission of failure of the socialist order by the rulers of the socialist countries was enough to attract massive development assistance from the advanced market economies and the multilateral institutions and agencies controlled by them. Formerly, inordinate delay used to occur in institutions such as the World Bank in processing the applications for development assistance. However, today, structural adjustment loans (which are but a euphemism for assistance for privatisation and marketisation) are sanctioned at amazing speed and with unprecedented enthusiasm.

The two immediate implications of the changes in the East European countries for the economies of the developing countries are: (1) the disappearance of the barter trade arrangements; and (2) the declining inflow of assistance from the developed countries. Owing to the lack of price competitiveness, the developing countries were never able to export to the hard currency countries in any significant manner. Hence, the socialist countries provided the major or only markets for the exports of the developing countries.

Combined with the disappearance of barter trade with the former socialist countries must be considered the declining flow of developmental assistance from the developed to the developing countries. The developed countries prefer to invest in the trasition economies which are according a red carpet welcome to such investment and where labour productivity is now considered to be very high.

As far as the debt crisis is concerned, the developing countries are increasingly getting into an inextricable tangle as is evident from the two increasing ratios, viz., (1) the ratio of external debt to GDP; and (2) the ratio of external debt to the export of goods and services.

The grave situation confronting the developing countries can be understood from the fact that their borrowings as proportions of their GDP have been increasing over the years. In sub-Saharan Africa, the proportion was as high as 71 per cent in 1990. In the case of a poor country, as in the case of a poor person, debts have a cumulative tendency to increase. Repayment of previously contracted loans would require further loans, probably from different sources. Experience till date shows that the economic impact of debt in a poor country is negative. In fact, debt may be the major source of economic backwardness. More often than not, the borrowing countries are not able to productively utilise the loans due to faulty identification and formulation of projects, absence of necessary institutional changes such as effective land reforms and redistribution of assets, concentration of political power in the hands of the ruling classes which emerged from the former feudal families, lack of new development ethos, excessively centralised nature of the decision-making process and so on.

Debt crisis, in a sense, shows the sickness of a country or a person. A sick person, most often, has a weak morale and is vulnerable. Any prescription by doctors will be unquestioningly accepted. Analogously, a heavily and chronically indebted country with few opitions, is wont to accept any conditionalities stipulated by a creditior. IMF and World Bank, the premier multilateral institutions operating on the basis of, and further strengthening, the rules of the game of the capitalist system, know this very well. They, accordingly, stipulate several conditionlities to the borrowers which are invariably developing countries. Compounding the vulnerability of the "debt problem developing countries" are what are called cross-conditionalities, that is the stipulation that a country borrowing from the IMF should accept not only the IMF conditionalities but also those of the World Bank and *vice versa.* It may be remembered in this context that by stipulating the conditionalities, the multilateral institutions are forcing the borrowing countries to reorder their priorities not on the basis of the problems and felt needs of the latter but on the basis of the perceptions of the former. These perceptions are, indeed, the perceptions of the advanced capitalist countries whose predilections and proclivities the multilateral institutions loyally reflect. In fact, it may not be very much wide of the mark to say that the IME and World Bank bureaucracy is the conduit for purveying the economic ideas and ideologies of the dominant market forces in the world.

Before we wind up this discussion on the global economic integration, it is pertinent to point out the increasing pace of differentiation of the developing countries so that we will be better able to appreciate the differential impact of the process on the economies of these countries. As has been rightly observed, till the first oil price hike in 1973, the economies of the developing countries were less differentiated. However, the oil crisis and the economic opportunities it offered to the oil exporting developing countries and the enormous cost escalation it entailed for the oil-importing developing countries drive a clear wedge between these two groups. The oil boom and the changes that occurred in the capital market consequent upon the mounting petro-dollar, resulted in the division of the developing countries into "debt-problem countries" and "others". The debt-problem countries, relying heavily on commercial creditors for external finance were forced to accept an external orientation of their economies with far-reaching implications as the restructuring of the economy at the dictates of the lenders inevitably resulted in the loss of economic sovereignty and also, as a result, political sovereignty. It needs to be borne in mind that from economic subservience to political subservience is only a short step.

However, ironically enough, this enforced external orientation did not result in any significant growth of exports. Exports from "debt-problem countries" rose only modestly from the depressed levels of the 1970s. Investment-GDP ratio registered a sharp decline. And total productivity registered a negative growth. On the contrary, despite the adverse terms of trade experienced since the outbreak of the debt crisis in 1982, " those countries that avoided debt-serving problems" could achieve enormous increases in their export growth, investment ratios and total productivity.

In view of the facts mentioned in the foregoing paragraphs, the divisions of the developing countries provided by the IMF seem to be relevant from the analytical as well as policy point of view. In addition to the division between "debt-problem countries" and "others", it gives various other categories as well. Of these, two seem to be particularly important in the present context. They are: (1) by region, and (2) miscellaneous. Under the division by region come the following: (a) Africa; (b) Asia; (c) Europe; (d) Middle East; and (e) Western Hemisphere. Miscellaneous groups are: (i) Sub-Saharan Africa, (ii) twelve major oil exporters, (iii) net-dèbtor fuel exporters; (iv) four newly industrialising Asian countries; (v) small low-income economies and (vi) fifteen heavly indebted countries. It goes without saying that the global economic integration will have different implications for the various categories of developing countries.,This would require them to adopt various policy packages suiting specific situations. However, the policy approach of the Bretton Woods twins and the ruling economic ideology aim at market-orientation and global integration.

6

THE EMERGING INTERNATIONAL INFORMATION ORDER : IMBALANCED, INEQUITOUS AND INTIMIDATING

Dr. N.A. Karim

The new world order, that is unfolding itself or, as some people believe, has already fully emerged, is highly tilted in favour of the developed countries of the West in all its dimensions—political, military, economic and technological, of the technological dimension the information technology aspect has an equal or even greater potential than the military aspect in determining the nature of the new order. The Gulf war was as much a clear case of demonstration of this potential as the enormous destructive power of the high-tech weapons that America and her industrially advanced allies alone possessed and which were cynically field-tested in the Gulf.

The US-led Western nations not only won the war but also triumphed in the more immoral disinformation blitzkrieg by their sheer high-tech monopoly over the existing information order. The world was flooded with US-controlled or US-supported Western news agency reports on the war as to how 'the international thug' Saddam Hussein's 'beastly soldiers' were carrying out 'shocking sex crimes' on women hostages after invading Kuwait. The environmental disaster brought about by this 'new Hitler' of Iraq was effectively driven home by repeatedly showing the image of a poor sea-bird soaked in oil slick and lovingly nursed back to life by a kindly American hand. On the other hand Pentagon extensively circulated video images of their bombs destroying only the military targets in Iraq completely blacking out the cruelties inflicted on the innocent Iraqi civilians who were savagely bombarded and killed by the multinational force as in the case of the most cruel bombing of al-Amiriya. All this was done ignoring the limit set by the Security Council Resolution No. 678. Pentagon itself, in perhaps an unguarded moment of euphoria, boasted that they 'reduced Iraq into a talcum powder bowl' in a week's work. It was thus in the Gulf war that the cynical and inhuman face of the new information order was first bared.

The term 'information imperialism' was first used by Urho Kekkonen, former President of Finland in 1973. The expression 'information colonialism' is only a verbal variation of the same concept which has become real and growing into menancing proportions. Though this imbalance in the informosphere was there ever since the Second World War it became a focus of attention in international conference only after the seventies. The need for a new international information order was voiced first by the nonaligned nations as information was vital for development and for the shaping of a just, meaningful international economic order. In the first flush of hope and enthusiasm for such an order, declarations were made, committees were formed and newspool was planned by the meet of non-aligned states.

In 1973 the fourth General Conference of the non-aligned countries held in Algiers adopted an Action Programme for the dissemination of information received from the member-countries and entrusted the task to the news agency TANJUG of Yugoslavia.Two years later more concrete proposals for the formation of a non-aligned media channel were discussed.

One such step was the establishment of regional centres for production and distribution of information. In 1976, at Colombo where the fifth Summit Conference of the non-aligned states was held, this idea of a new international information order (NIIO) was greatly stressed as an essentail prerequisite for a just and equitable world economic order. In the same year the Conference of Information Ministers of non-aligned nations held at New Delhi further discussed the information situation and came out with a Declaration and a resolution on an Action Plan for effective cooperation in the field of information and mass media. The sixth summit in Havana in 1979 'appreciated and hailed' the resolution adopted in the 33rd session of the UN General Assembly and commended the positive role of the UNESCO on the information question.

The UNESCO' resolution on the New World Information and Communication Order based on Mac Bride Commission Report was a modest attempt to"correct inequalities in the flow of information to and from developing countries and between those countries. Nearly 80 per cent of the world's newsflow emanated from the Western news agencies and 90 percent of the radio frequencies spectrum had been cornered by the developed countries.

The rest of the world is totally dependent on the Western media for information especially at a time of world crisis like the Gulf war. The bulk of world news is disseminated through the media of Western news organisations. The world's two biggest television news companies Visnews and WTN are owned and controlled by western organisations. The four big internatioal news agencies—Associated Press (AP), United Press International (UPI), Agence France Press (AFP) and Reuter—that control and regulate international newsflow are western, the first two American. They all work with a clear commitment to uphold and safeguard the western political, economic and military strategic interests. To reinforce this information stream there are such US vehicles as *Time* and *Newsweek* with world-wide circulation and readership.

In addition to these, there are reputed influential writers like Henry Kissinger whose syndicated articles on Western perceptions are read the world over. The developing countries like India proudly publish them and our intellectuals swallow whole their views on other Asians, Africans, Arabs and Latin Americans. Moreover, the editorials of reputed Western newspapers considerably influence public opinion in countries of their publication and abroad. For example, the editorials, and articles that are published in the *Times* (London) are read by a large number of goverment leaders and policy makers in third world countries. News and views published by Western print media are regularly reproduced in our newspapers as if they are gospel truth. A recent example is the news item that appeared in a prestigious American daily regarding Pakistan's nuclear capability. Our media made much of it and broadcast the item for several days as if it was a new revelation without even doubting about the American strategic motivation behind the item now.

There is another indirect influence of the Western media on the correspondents from developing countries based in Western capitals like London and Washington. They file their copies to their papers on the basis of what they get in such major news centres, which are always tinged with Western views and interests. In this situation, the UNESCO thought that this sort of extreme imbalance needed some corrective. Strange as it may appear to us, a furore was created by the then first world countries describing the effort of the UNESCO as a 'sinister move' to throttle the free flow of information and promotion of state intervention in the holy precincts of democracy.

Article 1 of the UNESCO Declaration states:

"The strengthening of peace and international under-standing, the promotion of human rights and countering of rcialism, apartheid and incitement to war demand a free flow and a wider and better balance and dissemination of information".

When it comes to real action according to the directives of the Declaration, the Western monopolists of information know only too well as to how to scuttle it and prevent its free flow. The US and UK went to the extreme extent of stopping their contributions to UNESCO and walking out of this world forum when they realised that this highly regarded world body is serious about correcting the imbalance. This hostility with the UNESCO ended only after its Director-General, M'Bow was eased out of office. Prominent Western newspapers like *New York Times* completely ignored the NAMEDIA conference held in Delhi in 1983 despite the fact that it was an important media event attended by several distinguished leaders of the Third World.

The demand for an equitable information world order continued in the eighties. The 37th session of UN General Assembly stated that it was conscious of the need for all to 'collaborate' in the establishment of a new world information order based on the free circulation and wider and better balanced dissemination of information guaranteeing the diversity of the sources and free access to information, and in particular, the urgent need to change the dependent status of the developing nations'. Moreover, the General Assembly session proclaimed in a ringing moral tone that the freedom of information is a fundamental right and is the touchstone of all other freedoms and that it requires 'the moral obligation to seek facts without prejudice and spread knowledge without malicious intent'.

But kaleidoscopic changes in international arena have overtaken these promising initial steps and soon wiped out the euphoric optimism created by them in the developing countries. The disappearance of the Soviet Union and the collapse of the socialist regimes of eastern Europe have made it possible for America and her Western allies to attempt to freeze the existing highly inequitable world order as the post-Cold War world they inherited is extremely convenient to perpetuate their exploitative economic interests and hegemonistic political ambitions. The developing countries are today comparatively silent on this vital issue due to various more pressing internal problems, and the information question has been put on the back burner as the thrust of their exertions today is narrowly economic.

Recently the issue has become a little alive in our country with media tycoons like Rupert Murdoch arriving on the scene with not fully disclosed plans to enter into our media world which, in any case, seems set for a major shake-up. On the recommendation of the first Press Commission, the Government of India had decided in 1955 that no foreign-owned newspaper should be allowed to publish in India, and newspapers and periodicals dealing mainly with news and current affairs should not be allowed to bring out Indian editions. Now the Government has received at least three requests from foreign publications. The *International Herald Tribune* has long been planning an Indian edition. The second one is a request for an Indian edition of *Time* in collaboration with the Living Media India, publishers of *India Today* with a 50 : 50 equity participation. The other is for a financial daily, a joint venture with the *Financial Times* of London. Will the entry of these giants give the Indian newspapers a much-needed competition or will it help information colonialism spread its tentacles to India is a matter to be carefully considered, and firm policy decisions are to be taken.

Communication technology has, in the last few decades, developed to such an astounding extent that we are now at a loss as to count it as a real blessing or a curse. This bewilderment is particularly great in the undeveloped and developing countries as they realise that the information technology which, like other technologies are monopolistically controlled by America and Western Europe, is being systematically and subtly, sometimes not so subtly too, used to serve their hegemonistic, political and economic interests. Countries of the South are at the receiving end in this onslaught through a calculated motivated information, mainly disinformation, campaign launched by the developed West.

At a popular level this new information technology is seen as a great blessing. Bored by the banal fare provided by our Doordarshan, the television viewers have now their fill of highly entertaining programmes beamed from commercial satellites. The number of such programmes is increasing. Beginning with CNN and Star TV now we have a rich variety to choose from with many more waiting to enter. The section of our society who views these programmes regularly imbibes unknowingly the political perceptions, social mores and cultural values of the West.

But there is another aspects to this technological blessing more dangerous than the cultural colonisation of the mind of those who are exposed to it. The recent major break-through in the information technology would not have been possible but for the active interest and generous funding of the military-industrial establishments of the West, particularly of Pentagon. They are always on the look out for more and more sophisticated weaponry. The multinationals seized this opportunity and mounted their R and D efforts to a high pitch which has resulted in this phenomenal advance in this area. Realising their great commercial potential these multinationals are exploiting the technology for civilian uses. This domination of the military-industrial complex of the developed countries over the information technology makes its core a guarded secret which will not be transferred to developing countries. In short, information has become a product with a prohibitive price-tag.

India and China are perceived as virgin media markets offering vast investment prospects. Murdoch with extensive media interests in Europe, North America, Australia and Hong Kong with an eye on China is now entering India with his main media vehicle News International acquiring 49.9 per cent stake in Bombay-based Asia Today which broadcasts Zee TV, a Hindi language entertainment channel. He has gambled wisely on new infromation technology be it in print media, book publishing or television. Today Murdoch has a stake in every important media development area and has built the world's biggest media conglomerate with a turn over of more than 15,000 crores.

Our ruling elite was excited by Murdoch's recent visit to this country though the media moghul wanted his appointments with the high and mighty on a discreetly subdued note perhaps for prudent tactical reasons. Due to internal and external compulsions, most of the developing nations are in a quandary at the moment. They do not now form a homogeneous group. Moreover, the internal elite are quite unlikely to weaken their political, economic and cultural links with the transnational interests. This is indeed a gloomy situation. The salvation lies in the realisation by the ruling class of the developing countries that their development strategy should not be based on seeking a few crumbs from the tables of the rich West. The present information imbalance and limitation of perspective is very dangerous for the future, particularly in this uncertain period of post - Cold War developments the final outcome of which is beyond any political prophecy.

Globalisation And De-empowerment

J. Prabhash

I. Introduction

The theoretical justification of modern liberal democracy rests on its claim to empower the people rather than a particular class or classes. The underlying assumption here is that in a democratic society people have a collective destiny in the formulation of which they have the last word. Thus, democratic governance postulates the finality of popular will. However, empowerment as a concept is not merely confined to an expression of popular will or organising people to articulate it. More significantly, it envisages greater democratic participation and involvement in the whole gamut of development and equipping people, mentally and materially, to discharge such positive roles in the system. The role of the State assumes salience here since empowerment as a multi-dimensional construct—particularly in its socio-economic dimensions—needs for its fulfilment and interventionist state. This is specifically so as it involves massive inputs of education, health, nutrition, housing and related living conditions, environmental enhancement and minimum access to land, water and common property resources.[1] An objective as this could be achieved only through the instrumentality of the State and, in modern times, to facilitate this it provides a cluster of socio-economic rights to the citizens. This testifies to the obvious centrality of the State in the process of empowerment.

As a testament of liberal democracy, the Constitution of India also seeks to institutionalise the above theoretical proposition in its body politic. Consequently an interventionist state has been established and its continued legitimacy has been pegged to its intent and capacity to ensure social, economic and political justice assuring the dignity of the individual. The ruling class which came to power in the years immediately following independence and a few decades thereafter also followed a host of policies which were supposed to realise this constitutional mandate. The spirit of planned development in the context of mixed-economy, agrarian reforms, various strategies worked out for poverty alleviation and agricultural development etc. was essentially this. These policies actually fell in the grey area between the two extreme ideological positions represented by Adam Smith and Karl Marx. It was a mix of socialism and capitalism and the stated objective was to ensure both growth and justice.

But the current economic thinking in the country represents a U-turn from the policies pursued so far. In fact, it is based on an altogether different praxis of development. Naturally such a cataclysmic change triggers a volley of questions: What is the possible impact of the new policy on different social classes, more particularly the subaltern sections of the society? Will it ensure a basic minimum to these people? Or conversely, will it only sharpen the existing exploitative structures of the society thereby adding density to the texture of inequality? Or will these sections be marginalised from the development process and eventually excluded from the system itself— a process of de-empowerment? This is an attempt to address these questions. Although the cacophony of arguments justifying Globalisation finds a hypnotic charm and a massive strength in such a drive and sees no cause to worry about the issues already raise, this paper takes a different course by presenting the alternative thesis— that the new matrix of development places the masses in a still grievous disadvantage by reinforcing the existing structures of domination and brutalizing their existence.

II. Globalisation : Nature and Propensity

Globalisation is coterminous with both Privatisation and Liberalisation. In fact, they form a union of trinity (commonly known as the

New Economic Policy) each reinforcing the other. As such Globalisation can be discussed only in relation to the other two. Together they are based on the premise that there are certain structural distortions in the Indian economy which, in the main, is a creation of the poplicies pursued by the Indian State since independence.[2] Consequently a change in the policies and paradigm of development is considered imperative. Changes in the global political and economic scenario also offered a powerful pretext in this regard.

As could be expected these policies intend to recast the Indian economy and re-orient the whole development process. Globalisation aims at fusing the country's economy with the world economy and abrogating or altering drastically commercial, exchange and investment regimes so as to ensure a 'level ground' for both domestic and foreign investors. In short, the domestic economy is opened up and is made susceptible to the changes in the global economy. Such a step, it is argued, would lead to a better and efficient utilisation of resources like capital and labour (due to competition), more participation in the global trade for domestic economy and larger foreign direct investment and collaboration.[3] Liberalisation and privatisation on their part seek to 'equip' the domestic economy to meet the new challenges involved in the opening-up process. In particular they aim to bring about reforms in critical micro economic areas such as industrial and trade licensing reforms, privatisation of public sector enterprises, institution of a flexible hire and fire policy and freeing of the financial secrtor[4]. Cumulatively these reforms entail a reduction in government employment and reduction or elimination of public expenditures (including consumer subsidies and many other social expenditures), increase in interest rates to attract capital inflow and raise domestic savings, drastic devaluation of domestic currency under fixed exchange rates, reduction of money supply, and emphasis on export crops and products as opposed to local food production or products intended for doemstic consumption, besides liberalisation of trade.[5] These, then, are the ineluctable ramifications of the above economic formulation, its cold rationale being free market and more profit. According to its pontiffs it leads to vigorous economic growth which brings within its train overall national development.

While some of the above claims are partially right, the rest are preponderantly, if not absolutely, wrong. Recall here that the new internationalists who champion the cause of globalisation pin their hopes about the replenishment of the national economy on greater participation of the county in international trade, increased foreign investment and more flexibility in technology transfer. However, the inner dynamics of such an argument offends the demands of elementary reasoning. It goes without saying that in a highly iniquitous world the terms of trade favour only the rich countries. Between the developed and developing coutries or capital rich and labour rich countries or in short between the lenders and the borrowers there cannot be, and never has been, any symmetry in business relations since the benefit predominantly goes in favour of the former[6]. Thus the effort at opening up the economy, only leads to opening the national market to the TNCs and MNCs for wanton exploitation.

Also there is not much reason to be over-enthusiastic about foreign investment and transfer of technology. The resource drain and huge financial commitment involved in this process apart, it won't also be in the enlightened interest of the domestic economy. A balanced historical view shows that everywhere and at all times foreign investment has been in those sectors of the economy which yield maximum returns. Social compulsions or needs of the home country have never been in the reckoning in this regard. Capital flight in the name of royalty, profit etc. to the metropolis adds another dimension to the issue. This would be much more easier now as exchange and investment regimes are being dismantled by the State. Similarly transfer of technology, unless negotiated prudently (chances for such a course are dim as the odds are against the developing countries) becomes detrimental to the nation's interest. Ponna Wignaraja succinctly points out this. He says:

> The highly capital-intensive and import substituting technology that continues to be implanted into the South with little social control or social conscience bears insufficient relation either to real factor endowment, particularly of labour, or to the existing knowledge system, or to the wide-range of technological choice available to the South. The entire process has been wasteful and the contradictions too sharp and numerous for any orderly form of management of the process as a whole for the real benefit of poor countries. Under these circumstances, for the South to keep asking for more of the same kind of aid is an irrational option.[7]

This has a daunting dimension as it upsets the dialogical relationship between technology and development, social needs of production and the factor endowment of a given society. Added to this issue is the redundant nature of the technology transferred. Various studies have already established that the technology passed on to the developing countries are often obsolete and also hostile to the environment. In such a context technology, instead of revolutionising the methods of production, only retards it and aggravates ecological problems. These ae some of the real issues which lurk behind the core economic justifications for Globalisation advanced by its advocates. One should take cognizance of these cramping limits of the policy as one proceeds to analyse its impact, especially its impact on various social classes and the democratic nature of the polity.

III. Globalisation and Social Classes

In a democratic polity a government policy is to be evaluated on the basis of its socially redeeming feature i.e., its capacity to bring about social transformation in tune with democratic ethos particularly socio-economic justice and equality. The expected change should also be beneficial to the majority of the population, greatest happiness of the greatest number as Utilitarians say. But the new development discourse hardly qualifies this criteria even by the most optimistic account. Explanation for this is not far to seek. A policy which speaks the language of a new mercantile ethos cannot fashion the economy in the enlightened interests of the masses. It favours only those who possess economic power and most advanced skills/learning to exploit the opportunities thrown open by it. The brute majority of the people who possess neither of these naturally end up as losers. As Nathan Gardels writes, "Only the archipelago of the connected classes that reside in every mega-city from Bombay to Sao Paulo will prosper from the new capitalist order. The rest of the ever swelling ranks of the lumpen planet face a fate worse than colonialism : economic irrelevance".[8] Thus it only widens the hiatus between the rich and the poor, in the process sharpening the socio-economic contradictions in the society. Studies conducted by the World Bank itself have corrborated this fact. For example, a 1974 study says, "It is now clear that more than a decade of rapid growth in underdeveloped countries has been of little or no benefit to perhaps a third of their population. Although the average per capita income of the Third World has increased by 50 percent since 1960, this growth has been unequally distributed among countries and socio-economic groups".[9] This would be more so in a country like India where the social terrain is highly iniquitous.

Though India witnessed substantial growth since independence its benefits have not significantly touched the poorest and the most needy sections with the result that the major contradictions inherent in its society still remain unresolved.[10] As a result of this even today as much as 50 per cent of the country's population lives under variously drawn poverty line,[11] and every second illiterate person in the world is an Indian.[12] The contradictions become more glaring as one looks at the pattern of land ownership. Gail Omvedt estimates that 70 to 80 percent of the total land in India is controlled by just 14 percent of the households.[13] The distribution of national income also follows more or less the same pattern. This is clear from juxtaposing the fact that while the country is ranked 15th in terms of GNP, it has the dubious distinction of being 106th in terms of per capita income.[14] The track record of the Indian State in other areas—providing adequate public health facilities, employment generation etc.—also leaves much to be desired. It is in such a society that the New Economic Policy is superimposed. Therefore, it only leads to unequal advantages for various classes. While it serves well the interests of the upper crest of the Indian society, it sharpens the disparities between them and the rest of the population. Indeed, this has been so ever since the focus of development shifted from social goals to technological goals and the prime instrument of development shifted from the State to the Market.[15] As public sector is wound up progressively and privatisation drive picks up momentum polarisation between various social classes becomes sharper still. Economic power comes to be concentrated in the hands of an ever decreasing number of landlord-money lender classes in the rural areas and financial cum industrial monopoly houses in the urban centres. The elite groups belonging to the intermediate classes—politicians, intellectuals and bureaucrats—also make moderate gains.

The asymmetry of economic power apart, the poor are affected in numerous other ways also. Inflationary pressures, under-employment, diminution of employment opportunities, withdrawal of government subsidies etc. which are the natural corollaries of the new policy will lead to a further deterioration of their living standards. Many studies including a recent one undertaken by the Asian Regional Team for Employment Promotion of the ILO corroborate this. According to the ILO study both under-employment and unemployment has increased in India since the adoption of the new policy package; further there has been a fall in real wages for casual labour in both urban and rural areas; and the incidence of poverty both in urban and rural areas has also increased, one of the major contributing factors for this being the steep increase in food prices by over 45 percent in three years between 1989-90 and 1992-93.[16]

Measures like devaluation of currency and other contractionary monetary and fiscal policies which are currently followed by the Government create inflationary pressure on the economy. This is a potential source of trouble for the poor and the working class as it increases the prices of essential commodities at a time when their real earnings are compressed. Here it is also important to note that employment by itself does not guarantee a specific level of real wage as the worker has no role in deciding the composition of output or the ratio of money wage to the price of his consumption basket.[17] Slashing of Government expenditure on social spendings like education, health, social security and subsidies on food also extracts its pound of flesh. This denies the poor even the little support mechanisms—public distribution system, health care, educational facilities etc. that are available for them to fall back on. The budgets presented by the Government of India and various State Governments since 1990 amply testify this. Going through them it becomes clear that expenditure on the above heads has fallen in real terms.

The NEP also holds the threat of aggravating the overall unemployment level. An important reason for this is the use of modern technology which by its very nature is labour displacing. It is true that it increases the quantum of production. But in the process it reduces avenues of employment by substituting machines for men. This of recent has given raise to a new phenomenon of 'jobless growth' even in western countries which in the past often faced acute labour shortage.[18] In a labour rich country like India, therefore, indiscriminate use of modern technology only spells disaster. Added to this, the closure of sick industrial units compounds the situation. Already it is pointed out that 40.5 lakh employees working in sick units in the private sector[19] and another 14.1 lakh working in public sector sick units are facing an uncertain future.[20] According to an estimate prepared by the ILO nearly eight million people would become unemployed in India in the period between 1992-95.[21] This would be a serious issue as the country already faces the problem of chronic underemployment and unemployment. At the same time the much trumpeted talk about safety net to cushion the impact of retrenchment has not clicked so far. The New Economic Policy thus places the lower strata of the society and even the middle strata including blue collar workers, and middle level bureaucrats in a distressing predicament. While it affects the very chances of survival of the lower classes it leads to a perceptible deterioration in the living standards of the middle class. But beyond all these problems of unemployment, sharpening economic contradictions and persisting poverty is at work a still deeper process—a clear shift in the paradigm of state intervention coupled with the emergence of a new philosophy of development—which has a far greater implication from a democratic perspective.

IV. Changing Paradigm of State Intervention and Emerging Philosophy of Development

As is already made clear at the outset, the theoretical underpinnings of liberal democracy assign a crucial role to the State. It is considered as a mediator in ameliorating the harshness of traditional social structures for the purpose of ensuring justice and equality, a protector of vulnerable peoples and liberator of oppressed and colonised populations and an engine of growth and development that would usher in a new civil order based on progress and prosperity and confer rights to life and liberty, equality and dignity, on the people at large.[22] In fact, it is this creative role that really binds the State with its citizens and gives legitimacy to it. But a major break in this pattern of relationship is discernible today.

Central to the new economic dispensation is a shift in the role of the State, particularly in its commitment towards the mass of the people from whom it supposedly derives its strength according to democratic tradition. No longer it is a positive instrument of social transformation or an autonomous entity acting above class interests or even a dispenser of justice. It is progressively vacating public spaces it has once occupied and consequently its functions are shrinking to such an extent that it is fast becoming a mere facilitator of capitalist acquisitiveness and an overseer of law and order. At the same time this does not mean a retreat of the State in line with the pristine *laissez faire* 'virtues'. Contrary wise it signifies a change in the paradigm of state intervention—a fundamental change in its welfare commitment and a transformation from a seemingly non-partisan state standing above classes and acting in the 'interest of the society' to a blatantly partisan state intent on smashing trade unions and winding up the social security system.[23] It is a sort of Corporate State which assigns priority to the interests of the landed gentry, the bourgeoisie and the bureaucratic-political elite combine. As such there would be hardly any place for distributive justice and much less the narrowing of economic disparities or even alleviating poverty. In this context, special care strategies for the disinherited classes, whether they be Scheduled Castes, Scheduled Tribes, women, children or minorities would be under constant scrutiny with a definite penchant for slimming down the quantum of assistance, if not abrogating it altogether.

Simultaneously, the new economic order also gives a new orientation to the whole process of development. Already it has lost its human touch. The idea that the objective of economic development is a narrowing of disparities and a general lifting of standards of living and livelihood or, as was the jargon in India, lifting millions from below poverty line is no more valued today.[24] Instead it has become an epitome of capitalist acquisitiveness. Mass production through hi-tech industrialisation rather than production by masses through appropriate technology is its motto. Interestingly enough, all these are done in the name of a false and facile dichotomy between development and justice. According to the appologists of the new order these twins never meet or co-exist.

Also the new development discourse hardly touches the vital issue of people's participation in the overall development process. Even the State is robbed of a significant part of its role in this regard. It is neither a facilitator of development nor even its overseer. This would be definitely so as most of the existing regimes on investment, exchange, commerce, and industry are dismantled giving greater latitude for private initiative in trade and industry. As a result social control over development is at a discount. It comes to be dominated by minority of techno-bureaucratic-political elite with TNCs and MNCs and indigenous big bourgeoisie pulling the strings from behind.

V. Environmental Dimensions

The environmental dimensions of the new economic thinking, particularly of the Globalisation component, also deserve serious consideration. Apart from the direct ecological hazards involved in the process—for example, pollution of land, air and water which are related to hi-tech industrialisation—it has another important aspect as it leads to a wanton exploitation of the natural resource base of the country, especially resources based on forest and sea. In human terms this has a disastrous consequence for certain groups of people like, the tribals, Scheduled Castes, traditional fishermen and such other groups who depend on them to eke out a living. Not only it disrupts their life style but the fast depletion of such resources deprives them of their very means of existence. They would also be torn away from their natural roots—as well as from their community and cultural ties—producing in them a sense of isolation.[25] This has an important side effect in that it upsets the sense of community found among people. Racall here that enviroment is one dimension around which a sense of unity and common purpose exists; it ties people together, including across class and other-caste and religious-barriers.[26] But decimation of nature through uncritical exploitation of its resources affects the harmony between man and his environment and between various groups of people. This eventually leads to a fragmentation of the people and their interests eroding the belief in a common destiny.

The daunting dimensions of the new economic thinking outlined above raise a fundamental question: What is the cascading effect of these dimensions on the democratic processes of the country? Surely, as poverty deepens and inequality gets accentuated, and as the State manifestedly becomes anti-poor and the thrust of the development process gets oriented accordingly, democratic spaces shrink.

VI. Subversion of Democracy

Poverty and inequality reinforce each other and accentuate socio-economic contradictions reducing democracy to a mere cariacture. As a result the power structure comes to be dominated more and more by those who wield economic power to the complete exclusion of the poorer sections of the society. Added to this is the problem arising out of centralisation of decision-making. Integration into the world market is only likely to centralise power and opportunities still further and restrict the scope of participation by the people in the development process or in governance and decision-making.[27] The development priorities of the nation and other vital issues affecting the people come to be decided by a new national-global elite combine in which international financial agencies and donor countries are also actively involved. Here it is important to note that the role of the Indian State itself will be minimal in this regard. This undermines the very principle of democratic accountability. When decisions are made by officials (not even politicians) often at international rather than national level, or by transnational corporations, or by politicians in other countries, the myth of accountability is difficult to sustain, particularly when the decisions that count are made in the corporate sphere, resulting in environmental disaster, loss of jobs, or financial risk.[28] Thus the system becomes less and less accountable to more and more people—the ever increasing number of the marginalised masses—and more and more accountable to less and less number of people—ever declining number of the new elite.

The paradigmatic shift in State intervention sets in motion another dangerous trend. It deprives the masses of all legitimate channels of ventilating their grievances. There is a decline in the importance of the State not only as a catalyst of development but also as an instrument for redressing grievances, providing correctives where injustices have occurred and processing demands of the deprived and disinherited sections of society.[29] Though this is partly due to its insensitivity towards their demands, more importantly it stems from the decline of democratic institutions of the State. As centralisation gets under way, institutions which are responsible to the people and which reflect their interests get marginalised. Already in India, there is much talk about the decline of legislature. Globalisation helps to reinforce this trend and adds a new dimension to this process as even the executive government loses much of its leverage in decision-making. The judiciary is also affected by this rot. It also declines in importance and effectiveness. There will be an increasing tendency either to disregard its decisions, or side track or overcome it by resorting to constitutional amendments. A keen observer of Indian politics could notice that already the strictures passed by the judiciary against governmental deviance—especially in matters affecting the poor—command little respect from the ruling class. More serious than this, there is an alarming tendency on the part of this class to consider judiciary as an intruder in its legitimate sphere of activity as and when decisions inconvenient to it are pronounced. All these generate an explosive situation in which the masses find themselves defenceless both materially and institutionally against the assault as well as exploitation of the dominant classes. This is a situation which a democratic State can hardly brook.

VII. Conclusion

It is within the above formative context that the ways and practices of power in the country are going to be shaped and moulded. As such there is no place for any great expectation that the ordinary masses would be represented in the system in any meaningful way or that the system would show any degree of concern for their interests. For the poor, therefore, the emerging order spells marginalisation, not only economically but socially and politically as well. They are not only excluded from the so called 'fruits of development' but also from the community and the social structure, the environment and the natural resource base and the State and its power structure.[30] They are deprived of their democratic rights and positive freedoms and do not have even a supportive role in the system. Disembodied and disenfranchised they become just like a cog in a machine. Here Indian democracy is emptied of its greatest claim that it seeks to empower the people as against a particular class or classes. Contrariwise, the unfolding reality points towards a distressing scenario in which the brute majority of them are progressively de-empowered.

References

1. Rajni Kothari, *Growing Amnesia: An Essay on Poverty and Human Consciousness*, New Delhi: Viking, 1993, p.73.
2. According to the advocates of Globalisation, state intervention in production and distribution is a major source of distortion of the Indian economy. In the name of equality, social justice and the like it has arrested the productive energies of the Indian bourgeoisie which factor is responsible for a slump in production and growth, they argue.
3. Anup Sinha, "Development: The New Agenda in a Changing Global Scenario", *Asian Studies*. Vol. 10, 1992, pp.30-31.
4. M.A. Oommen, "Bhagwati—Srinivasan Paper on 'India's Economic Reforms': A Critique," *Mainstream*, Vol. XXXI, No.46, 25 September 1993, p.11.

5. Michael J. Obadan and Bright U. Ekuerhare, "The Theoretical Bases of Structural Adjustment Programme in Nigeria : An Appraisal", International Social Science Journal, No. 41, May 1989, p.211 in Jennifer M. Coston, "An Exploration of the Theoretical Underpinnings of Structural Adjustment", *The Indian Jorunal of Political Science,* Vol. 53, No.2, April-June 1992, p.184.
6. K.S. Krishnaswamy, "On Some Issues in Globalisation", IASSI *Quarterly,* Vol. II, No.1, July-September 1992, p.15.
7. Ponna Wignaraja, "Rethinking Development and Democracy", in Ponna Wignaraja (ed.), *New Social Movements in the South: Empowering the People,* New Delhi: Vistaar Publications, 1993, pp.8-9.
8. Nathan Gardels, International Herald Tribune, 14 April 1993 in Mathew Horsman and Andrew Marshall, *After the Nation-State, Citizens, Tribalism and the New World Disorder,* London: Harper Collins Publishers, 1994, p.227.
9. Hollis Chenery et al (eds.), Redistribution with Growth, Oxford: OUP, 1974, N.pag. in C.T. Kurien, *Growth And Justice: Aspects of India's Development Experience,* Madras: OUP, 1992, pp.7-8.
10. Kothari, op.cit., p.141.
11. Lloyd I. Rudolph and Susanne Hoeber Rudolph, *In Pursuit of Lakshmi: The Political Economy of the Indian State,* Chicago: The University of Chicago Press, 1987, p.10.
12. J. D. Sethi, *Character of the Indian State: A Non-Marxist View,* Shimla: Indian Institute of Advanced Studies, 1992, p.63.
13. Gali Omvedt, "Capitalist Agriculture and Rural Classes in India" in Berch Berberoglu (ed.), *Class, State and Development in India,* New Delhi: Sage Publications, 1992, p.104.
14. Rasheeduddin Khan, *Bewildered India: Identity, Pluralism, Discord,* New Delhi: *Har-Anand Publications, 1994, p.47.*
15. Kothari, *op.cit.,* p.21.
16. D. Bandyopadhyay, "Economic Reforms and Constitution", *Mainstream,* Vol. XXXII, No.21, 9 April 1994, p.32.
17. Kanta Ranadive, "Market, Democracy and Unequal Relations", *Economic and Political Weekly,* Vol.XXIX, No. 5, 29 January 1994, p.PE-6.
18. This is a situation in which even when output increases, employment lags way behind. One of the important reasons identified for this phenomenon is the application of labour saving technology in production. For details see UNDP, *Human Development Report;* Delhi: Oxford University Press, 1993, p.36.
19. S.S. Mehta, The Implication of the Exit Policy, Ahmedabad: Gandhi Labour Institute, 1992, N. pag. in Ajith Kumar Singh, "Social Consequences of New Economic Polity with Particular Reference to Levels of Living of Working Class Population", *Economic and Political Weekly,* Vol. XXVIII, No. 7, 13 February 1993, p.284.
20. Singh, *op.cit.*
21. Kavaljith Singh, "Imparting a 'Human Face' to Structural Adjustment", *Mainstream* Vol. XXX, No. 41, 1 August 1992, p.15.25.
22. Kothari, "Masses, Classes and the State", in Wignaraja (ed.), *op.cit.,* p.62.

23. Prabhat Patnaik, "A Note on the Political Economy of the 'Retreat of the State", *Social Scientist*, Vol. 20, No. 11, November 1992, p.49.
24. Kothari, Growing Amnesia, *op.cit.*, p,20.
25. Ibid., p.114.
26. Ibid.
27. Ibid., p.59.
28. Horsman etal., *op.cit.*, p.221.
29. Kothari, Growing Amnesia, *op.cit.*, p.21.
30. Ibid., p.86.

7

Institutional Aspects of Economic Liberalisation : A Vision of the Co-Operatives

V. Nanda Mohan and P.N. Sankaran ***

Introduction

In their search for appropriate socio-economic forms of organisation for the construction of a new society the political leaders of the Third World came upon the idea (or revival of the idea already gaining acceptance during the colonial period as in India) of Co-operatives with European origins. The optimistic hope that a transfer, in a suitably modified form of the appropriate co-operative types, to the developing countries would lead to swift economic growth with socio-cultural adaptation, are clearly expressed in the papers contributed to the IIIrd International Co-operative Congress (Report of the Third International Conference on Co-operative Science, Marburg, 1960). Although the number of co-operatives multiplied rapidly in the Third World, numerous failures and disappointments could not be overlooked (Crisis of the Co-operative Societies in Policies of Development, Dulfer (ed), 1975). For example, the powerful position of the Registrar of Co-operative Societies paved the way for the officialisation of the co-operatives and even in the Third World, we find the dilemma of the co-operatives—members desire for self-determination and the technical/organisational tendency towards centralisation of decisions.

* Head Department of Futures Studies, University of Kerala, Tribandrum.

** Lecturer Department of Economics, University College, Trivandrum.

In the seventies and eighties the co-operatives has to assert themselves both in the industrialised and developing countries, in an unusually turbulent environment vitiated by failure of the Bretton Woods System in 1973, the Oil Crisis, changing outlook to the role of the state (leading to liberalisation and encouragement to private sector initiatives). In tune with the changes in the global environment and growing internal contradictions, structural adjustments in the national economy have been a common feature in all parts of the world and this has swept over the co-operative form of economic organisation also. As far as co-operatives are concerned, there is an emerging realisation that the primary role of government is not to control (or regulate) their activities, but to provide a conducive policy and business environment for their operations (Hussi et al, 1993, p. XV). In India, where the policy of liberalisation and reforms are under way, to integrate our economy with the global environment, the outlook for the co-operatives in the 21st century has to be visualised against the backdrop of the process of liberalisation that is sweeping across many countries. The present paper tries to highlight the role, prospects and problems of the co-operatives in the 21st century against the background of the process of globalisation and market liberalisation with special reference to India.

2. Co-operatives—Defined

From a technical point of view a co-operative is a legally recognised form of association of persons, owned by its memebers, whose main principles include voluntary membership to achieve a common end and equal voting rights for each member. Not all organised groups are 'co-operatives'. The ILO has summarised the essential characteristics of a co-operative as an association of persons who have voluntarily joined together to achieve a common objective through the formation of a democratically controlled organisation, making equitable contribution to the capital required and accepting a fair share of the risks and benefits of the undertaking (ILO, 1966 ; Young Johns, 1977). The generally accepted principles of co-operative business are: open and voluntary membership, democratic control, limited interest on share capital, the promotion of member education and equitable distribution of economic gains. There are different kinds of co-operatives in developing countries. The most prominent are agricultural input supply, marketing, and savings and credit co-operatives. Consumer, housing and handicrafts co-operatives also exist in a number of countries.

3. Co-operative and the Changing Environment

a. The market failure argument

Economists have drawn attention to the failures of the market mechanism in the achievement of full employment, distributive jusitce, efficiency and growth. Market mechanism also fails in cases like the provision of public goods and services, merit goods, etc., where externality, indivisibility and free-riding tendencies reduce their provision to a socially sub-optimal level. On the assumption of market failure, there is a general tendency to opt immediately for a switch to services supplied by the state. Institutional solutions occupying a kind of third sector between market and state are, in contrast, scarcely taken in to consideration (Hanusch, 1985). Only recently are people beginning to ask whether it might not be possible to reduce the increase in state expenditure by entrusting a proportion of the state services to institutions not belonging exclusively either to the free market economy or the state. According to Hanusch, the provision of public goods could even be far more important, in future to co-operative supply forms than those numerous business spheres where co-operatives are already active alongside private enterprise (Ibid, p. 70). In such a co-operative setup the bureaucracy is strictly supervised by the users who are members of the society.

b. The market liberalisation argument

Governments in many countries like India are now fastly moving towards a market-oriented economic strategy. There is, as yet, little empirical evidence of the impact of a deregulated pricing and marketing regime on the market share of the co-operatives. However, the indications are that co-operatives due to their tradition of operating in a regulated market have difficulties in adjusting to a competitive market environment. A world Bank study has concluded that the ongoing dismantling of the regulated marketing and pricing system in Africa accentuates the need as well as the potential for co-operatives. Co-operatives can serve as a countervailing power to other private sector enterprises and thereby safeguard farmers against unfair trading practices (Hussi, et al, 1993, p. 31). Clearly there is a need for revision of co-operative development policies to bring them into line with the requirements of a liberalised economy and the concept of co-operative as private business organisations. Past experience strongly demonstrates a negative correlation between the degree of government administrative control of co-operatives and the economic success and sustainability of co-operative societies.

According to Taimni economic liberalisation and the structural adjustment programmes (redefinition of the role of the state and the macro-policy frame) are likely to affect the co-operatives in two ways viz. (i) fundamental change in the state co-operative relations in respect of the flow of public funds as loans and subsidies, measures providing protection and reservation for co-operatives and the laws governing co-operatives, (ii) following the wider changes in the economy, the community will demand better and efficient services from co-operatives than what they offer now (Taimni, 1993). In the context of the trends towards economic liberalisation in Sub-Saharan Africa, it is maintained that the content of co-operative reform should be to give autonomy to the co-operatives and to reduce the powers of the Registrar of Co-operatives to intervene into their management. The duties of the Registrar should be restricted to registration, arbitration and dissolution of co-operatives. (Hussi, et al., 1993, p. 37). Three policy issues have been identified as of central importance for the development of co-operatives in the liberalisation process. These are (a) policies regulating government supervision of control; (b) co-operative legislation; and (c) policies determining the business operations of co-operatives. In the World Bank Technical Paper Number 199 (May 1993), operational guidelines are given for the successful functioning of co-operatives in the present global trend of liberalisation, The most significant guideline being the explicit recognition of the co-operatives as private enterprises which are formed and managed by their members and which are not subject to intervention by government authorities in their internal management.

4. Economic Reforms and Co-operative Development: The Indian Scenario

a. Size and problems of the co-operative sector

The co-operative movement was started in India in the first decade of the twentieth century. Since then, it has grown in stature and extent of coverage. With an enormous number of 3.53 lakh co-operative societies, a membership of 16 crores and a total working capital of Rs. 70,000 crores, it is one of the largest in the world. Though Agricultural Credit Societies constitute the most significant segment in the co-operative system, their presence is notable in fertilizer distribution, milk, sugar and oil-seeds production, spinning and weaving, marketing and storage of agricultural produce, fisheries, housing and even in the promotion of tourism. The Indian co-operatives are mainly state sponsored and the basic act framed in 1904 by the colonial regime continues to govern their working without much modification. It is alleged that the act by conferring overwhelming powers on the Registrar has been institutionalising government regulation over the co-operatives. Under the co-operative act the Registrar assumes the guise of the Trinity—Brahma, Vishnu and Maheswara—with powers to Create, Sustain and Destroy. (Dubashi, 1993). Co-operatives in countries like India have been placed under the 'bureaucratic model' destined to be within an inescapable vicious circle of 'dependency trap', of government control, politicisation, poor performance leading to greater dependence on government. (Seetharaman and Mohan, 1985).

b. Co-operative development: Issues and prospects

When the policy of economic liberalisation and market regime are fully got implemented, no doubt, the state will have to withdraw from sponsorship and control of co-operatives and limit itself to promotional functions. It would be interesting, therefore, to examine the present state of Government measures and policies on co-operative development. Following the experience of the African countries we may look at the issue from the point of view of policies regulating government supervision of control, co-operative legislation and policies determining the business operations of co-operatives. It would be convenient to discuss issues one and two together as they are mutually reinforcing.

It is believed that the primary reason for co-operative paralysis, if not failure, is the overwhelming government presence, regulations and regimentations (Kurian, 1993). The continued application, without substantial amendments, of the age-old colonial co-operative laws, the bureaucracy weilding unlimited and loosely defined powers from them, erosion of co-operative values, education, training, etc. have been the factors of co-operative failure. It seems that we are very much late in getting the co-operative values restored and procedures modified. Unfortunately very little positive reform measures have come out for the development of co-operatives in the wake of the strategy of economic liberalisation. In fact, one is at a loss to find the near total neglect and absence of a clear vision about the future of co-operatives under the liberalised economic scenario. For example, in the VIIIth Five Year Plan document there is a hardly any reference to the co-operatives. The position today is that neither the co-operatives nor the co-operators know where exactly they stand in the economic order. Advocates of the movement hold the view that a strong co-operative sector is indispensable to protect the interests of farmers, artisans and weaker sections from the exploitative private sector, thriving under the liberalised economic policy (Vishwanathan, 1993, p. 2). In the event of commercial banks withdrawing from priority sector advances as recommended by the Narasimham Committee, the co-operative credit agencies will be the only agencies to fill the gap. The lack of commitment of the Government to co-operative reform may be noted from the fate of the Ardhanreeswaran Committee (1987). `The Report of the Committee on Co-operative Law for Democratisation and Professionalisation of Management in Cooperatives' was rejected.

Despite the general mood of disenchantment and lack of vision about the co-operatives, some positive and helpful development have also appeared in their horizon. A Model Law of Co-operatives has been framed in 1993 by a Committee constituted by the Planning Commision. It envisages integrated, despoliticised, and authonomous co-operatives free from government participation in share capital; the co-operatives are empowered to launch subsidiaries and joint ventures as done by purely commercial enterprises. Yet another significant suggestion is to limit the role of the Registrar to registration and liquidation of societies. The need for the change (in co-operative law) has become all the more urgent with the liberalisation of the industry enabling the private sector and even multinationals to operate without fetters (Bhatt, 1993).

We have seen that policies on co-operatives as business organisations constitute a vital ingredient in the reform of co-operatives in a liberalised setup. Recently the government has formulated a National Policy on Co-operation to revitalise the sector and make the agencies self-reliant. The New Agricultural Policy also envisages the active participation of the co-operatives in the processing of agricultural produce and development of the non-farm sector. There is also a move to constitute a development fund for co-operative education, an agency to tap the insurance business potential of the co-operatives and an infrastructure for international transfer of technology and movement of goods under the co-operative umbrella. To facilitate better deployment of surplus funds in the credit system and co-ordinate its activities at the apex level the National Co-operative Bank of India (NCBI) has been registered under the Multi-state Co-operative Societies Act. However, none of the measures outlined above are capable of improving the status of co-operatives to assume their new role as business organisations. It is true that the Pant Committee (set up to suggest measures for implementing the recommendations made by the Agricultural Credit Review Committee, 1989) has proposed the initiation of a process of business development planning in primary agricultural co-operatives. However, little progress has been made by the proposed drive for business development planning. The Report of the Committee on the Financial System (1991) did not even make a mention of the co-operative credit system. Thus even after two years of economic reforms and market-oriented development thrust, the co-operatives are yet to assume development orientation with modified business strategy.

5. Emerging Profile of Co-operatives: Alternative Approaches

In their search for a vision of co-operatives in the 21st century, economists have hinted at different models/strategies of growth. On the basis of trend analysis of co-operative development and experience of other countries it is argued that three distinct types of co-operatives might emerge in India, viz., commercial co-operatives, government co-operatives and self-help co-operatives. Commerical co-operatives will function like private business firms except for co-operative principles but will not have any long-term association with the state. Urban co-operative banks, sugar factories, hospitals, and Department Stores, Housing Societies, etc., may be placed under the commercial co-operatives. Government Co-operatives will be agencies (like IFFCO, KARIBCO, Credit, Marketing and Handloom societies) acting as instruments of the state for larger social purpose. Self-help co-operatives (examples are Rural Women Savings Groups, Industrial Workers' Co-operatives) will be characterised by value-based orientation, informal character, smaller size and premium on participation (Taimni 1992).

In a fully liberalised setup concessions, subsidies, reservations, protection, etc. presently offered to the co-operatives will be minimised. Conditions of massive poverty, inequality and unemployment, however, justify their continuation. One is yet to see the probable impact of liberalisation on the above problems over time. Given the magnitude of the economic problems involved and the complex socio-political dimension thereto, it would be advisable for the co-operatives to get prepared for the challenges of liberalisation. We maintain that the focus of a vision for the co-operatives should be based on continuation, during the initial phase (not by the Government but by the co-operatives themselves) of concessions, subsidies and protection of those co-operatives catering to the less previleged. The cost of such an arrangement may be met from a national co-operative development fund set up and subscribed to regularly by profit making/urban centred commercial co-operatives, with substantial initial contribution by the government. The weak co-operatives must emulate lessons from successful co-operatives; more importantly, the better performing cooperatives' technology and management need be copied. Also groups of co-operatives which are in the same line of activity can be formed whereby successful co-operative can be elected as the group leader. By developing such co-operative groups, the spirit and message of co-operative culture get diffused—even the younger generation get attracted by the movement.

6. Conclusions

Co-operatives are important avenues for social change, democratic progress and community development in general. They are, however, essentially business enterprises. The experience of the countries with relatively well-developed co-operative structure has shown that agricultural support and other services offered to members on commercial basis ensured sustainable co-operative development. To render better services to their members and to compete successfully with the profit-seeking private enterprises the co-operatives in the liberalised setup need to build a capacity to assume responsibility for promotional and development functions which hitherto have been vested with government departments. However, judging from the lack of vision and inadequate policy support for the revitalisation of the co-operatives so far in the emerging scenario of liberalisation, their prospects and capabilities to serve as a countervailing power to the private sector seem very bleak. The social and economic cost of failure of the co-operatives in the new dispensation would be very high, given the extent of rural poverty and unemployment prevalent in India. Our experience in India indicates that liberalisation, though it may be highly appealing, literally and intellectually, may provide a recipe which is too costly to afford for the weaker sections of the community. Co-operatives, therefore, face a challenge in India; the speedy dismantling of government support and direction without adequate and timely policy initiatives to make the decks safe and viable for them may spell their disaster and possibly for the poor millions depending mostly on their services. It would be proper at this juncture to make co-operative movement innovative.

References

Bhatt, Arunkumar (1993), Model Law for Co-operatives, the Hindu Daily, July 29.

Dubashi, P.R. (1993), "Co-operatives in a New Era of Liberalisation", National Bank Review, Sep. Vol. 8, No. 7, p. 35.

Dulfer, Eberhard and Hamm, Walter, (1985), (ed.) Co-operatives in the Clash Between Member Participation, Organisational Development and Bureaucratic Tendencies, Quiller Press, London.

Dulfer, Eberhard (1985), "The Co-operatives Between Member Participation, the Formation of Vertical Organisations and Bureaucratic Tendencies, An Introduction to the Theme", in Dulfer and Walter (1985) ed., Co-operatives, Quiller Press, London, pp. 1-15.

Hanusch, Horst (1985), "Market and Bureaucratic Failure as a problem of Self Help Development" in Dulfer, Eberhard and Hamm Walter, (1985) (ed.) Co-operatives, Quiller Press, London, pp. 57-75.

Hussi, Pekka et al. (1993), The Development of Co-operatives and Other Rural Organisations: The Role of the World Bank, World Bank Technical Paper No. 199, Africa Technical Department Series, The World Bank, Washington, D.C.

ILO, (1966), Developing Countries, Recommendation, No. 127, Geneva Switzerland.

Institute for Co-operation in Developing Countries, University of Marburg, Germany (1962), Report on the Third International Conference on Co-operative Science, Marburg/Lahn 1960, Gottingen 1962.

____(1975), Crisis of the Co-operative Societies in Policies of Development, Dulfer, E (ed).

Seetharaman S.P. and Mohan, N. (1985) "Organisation Building in Co-operatives—A Frame Work", in Dulfer & Hamm (1985) ed., Co-operatives, Quiller Press, London, pp. 201-215.

Taimni K.K. (1992) "Co-operatives under Deregulated Market Economy" NCDC Bulletin, Vol. 26, June-Aug Vol. 2-3, pp. 13-15.

Vishwanathan, B.S. (1993), "Impact of New Economic Policy on Co-operatives'. Land Bank Journal, Vol. 31, March, Issue 3, pp. 1-4.

Youngiohns, B. (1977), Co-operative Organisation : An Introduction, ITP Ltd.

8

The Role of National Security in the Search of Vision for the Future India

Dr. H. K. Srivastava *

Every nation strives to provide for its citizens a peaceful and a "Good Life."[1] The vision of peace and a "Good Life" have motivated elites and statesmen of a state to ensure that their state achieves that status in the comity of nations that other states are deterred to disturb the peaceful tranquillity and the welfare of their citizens. Nehru's "World Order Idealism"[2] searched ways and means so that threats from the collective global problems, like poverty, imperialistic domination, ideology and religious fundamentalism, hegemony of nuclear powers, and so on, do not impact India. Nehru, therefore, strived to bring about a humanitarian world order through disarmament, moral education, international law, and international institutions. How Nehru felt dejected and humiliated after 1962 Sino-Indian War is a well known fact. Nehru in the pursuit of his ideals in a nuclear world of the 20th century failed to recognise that his ideal and his vision could be only achieved if the state 'survived', that it retained its power to protect its members, and provided for them the conditions of a good life. As Croce had put it: "History does not acclaim as heroes those who have sacrificed their native land to an ideal, but rather condemns them for having subordinated the interests of the state to any other motives however generous."[3] Thus, survival of the state is the highest responsibility of those who conduct the affairs of the state. This survival can only be achieved if the

* Dr. H. K. Srivastava, M. Sc., Ph.D Principal, NDA (Retd.), Shahyog Building Narbada Road, Jabalpur - MP India - 482 001

security of the state is sound and strong and the state possess the ways and means to deter other states from interfering and disturbing the on-going processes of a peaceful development within the state.

In a technology-dominated world environment, no nation, except at its own peril, can fail to comprehend the new thinking and concepts that have evolved because of technological revolution and the numerous fields it has impacted.[4] A realisation of these concepts alone can channelise the national efforts towards sophistication and innovation at the indigenous technological levels, and, at the same time, bring an awareness of the perils nation may face, regionally and globally, by ignoring them, or remaining innocent about them.[5]

This paper will attempt to discuss how through the process of Military-Technology-Industry (MTI) development and improvement, the Indian vision of peace and 'Good Life' can be reached and possibly achieved.

National Power

National power is a function, of material assets, e.g., (a) geographical size and location, (b) size of population, (c) economic strength and development of science, technology and industry, (d) social and political organisations and institutions, and (e) military capability, including the size and structure of armed forces, quality and quantity of weapon systems doctrines and strategies of employment of military forces. These are the five determinants which are considered important for national power.[6] National power has been discussed extensively in the west.[7,8] Its abstract nature is still a matter of debate. It is, however, realised that the military strength and technological base have a much greater, though not absolute, role in national power. "The Soviet Union, like Tsarist Russia before it, was a lopsided great power,"[9] because it was economically weak though politically and militarily strong with a rich territorial endowment. Even the Russia of today has enough military capability, yet it cannot keep pace with rapidly advancing technologies. Russia was and will remain, therefore, "Surrounded not by invincible armies but superior economies."[10] Germany, Japan, China, South Korea, Taiwan etc., are some examples which show what determines national power, yet nations may not have a superpower status, or even recognised in the accepted sense as a powerful nation.

India has since 1960s came to be recognised as a regional power. It has amongst the five determinants of the national power size, population, and political strength, yet its MTI base has not up to date reached that level which can "hold off" intransigent neighbouring nations, liek Pakistan from interfering in its internal affairs, or major powers, like the USA, intervening in its political management (refer to recent Malottomania and continuing Raphelophobia about NPT and Kashmir).

In the 21st Century, India as a regional power can only reach its vision of power, peace and "Good Life" if the changed nature of war, new concepts about nuclear weaponry, impact of 'spin-on', 'spin-off' and duel technologies, and the role of evolving non-nuclear technologies is understood and attempts made to acquire them to the extent economic, technological, and industrial infrastructure permits.

The Changed Nature of Warfare

It was believed that the World War II was truly "the war to end wars". But, numerous wars were fought on the peripheries, although revolutionary technological innovations, chiefly weapon innovations, ensured that peace, though a troubled one, prevailed at the centre of international politics. These technological revolutions have greatly enlarged war concepts, both nuclear and conventional, and brought in new doctrines. They also brought in a kind of undistinguishable weapon continuum,[11] creating a great deal of uncertainty. As a sequel, national defence planning moved away from threat-specific to a mission-specific framework.

Moreover, the Gulf War showed that war fighting has already extended into the 'fourth dimension.' Space supported war making capabilities were fully displayed and deployed in this war. The long range capabilities, aided by ultra sophisticated reconnaissance, surveillance, and target acquisition systems have brought war, according to Singh, to the threshold of the fifth dimension, that of time itself.[12]

Nuclear Weapons

The changed nature of war was heavily influenced by the coming of the nuclear weapons. While technological innovations in conventional weapons intensify competition, with nuclear weapons, it is not so, except under an extraordinary breakthrough. As Bernard Brodie put it: "Weapons that do not have to fight their like do not become useless because of the advent of newer and superior types."[13] A nuclear country can follow a deterrent strategy no matter what other countries may do. The Soviet and the US relationship is a classical example of the deterrent strategy practice. Under this strategy only a small second-strike force is needed, large enough to sustain a first strike and able to retaliate with a few warheads, the Chinese approach. Moreover, a trip-wire conventional force is needed under deterrent strategy.[14] A large conventional force becomes irrelevant. This aspect of the nuclear weaponry India understands fully but is not in a position to practise for reasons other than military or economics.

One of the most profound gains of nuclear weaponry is that it favours *status quo* countries by enabling them to concentrate attention on their economics rather than on their military forces. By relying on deterrence, a state can concentrate on turning resources in the military sector of its economy to civilian uses. Still more, nuclear weaponry increases the frontiers of national economic capabilities. Though nuclear weapons do not make states into great or major powers, e.g., Britain, France, (new) Russia, but beause no state can challenge: such a nuclear state, they diversify their economic capabilities beyond their frontiers.

By stretching the above arguments to some extent, one can say that India's nuclear capabilities and growing competence in the nuclear field acted as a deterrent to challenge it during the last 22 years and under the nuclear capability umbrella India could advance its technological and industrial base so much so that to-day by liberalising its economic policies. India has greatly widened its economic frontiers. It is for Indian economists to decide whether India's economy belongs to the intermediate level of development in terms of Frederick List's classification,[15] or it is forced to slavishly follow "the School's free-trade theory,[16] or it is partly following Shinohara's" infant industry protection policies,[17] or the so-called Japanese "strategic trade theory". Be as it may, Walt's assertion that "Because nuclear weapons widen the range of economic capabilities within which great powers and would-be great powers can effectively compete, the door to the great power club will swing open" on a knock on it appears to be not only correct but also substantiated by world events.[18] It can-not be said with affirmation that India's sticking to its 'nuclear option' argument is based on such premises or otherwise. But Indian tenacity bore fruits. India is a recognised regional power. Had it not been so, Prof. Thomas Thornton of George town and John Hopkins Universities would not have acknowledged in his testimony before the House at Asia and Pacific hearing on the Administration's foreign assistance request that "We (the USA) need to accept the fact that we have very little leverage on either India or Pakistan. We are not in a position to apply military pressure on them....." He also suggested that the USA should lower its posture in dealing with the non-proliferation and missile issues.[19]

There are other undisputed gains to a country with nuclear weaponry. For example, a country, say like India, with much-less economic capability of a leading producer can easily compete militarily if it adopts a *status quo* policy and a deterrent strategy. Possessing nuclear capabilities deters attacks on a country's vital interests because nuclear weapons are no longer useful for taking other's territory or for defending one's own. As nuclear capability serves that end and no other, peace has held between India and Pakistan for the last 22 years and between the USA and the Soviet Union for the last five decades.

The American attempts to browbeat India over NPT is based purely on above realities of nuclear weaponry and nuclear capabilities. The Indian vision is also firmly rooted on these realities and will not be surrendered, one hopes, under duress. More awareness of such nuclear realities is needed to be propagated within the Indian masses.

New Technologies

It is a well recognised fact that the 'spin-off' impacts of innovations in military technology were quite strong on the civilian technology. However, in recent years, civilian technology has innovated at a very fast rate in the realm of automation, cybernation, and integration. This has resulted in increasingly recognisable 'spin-on' benefits to military. Computer-aided design and manufacturing has reached that level of sophistication and confidence that quite a few engineering and testing can be done with computer without the whole system going field testing. The US B-2 bomber never went through a prototype stage but to direct production. In future, many such complicated engineering feats would see a direct production phase. There are also trends to extend the life of existing systems (weapons and non-weapons both) and upgradatioin of software rather than hardware subsystems. Thus, systems may remain stored or 'frozen', so to say, in a software state and directly put to production on need basis.

The innovations in weapon system as a result of 'spin-on,' 'spin-off', and duel technologies have provided a variety of options for uses. One set of weapons can deny space and time, another can attack enemy economic and power targets, some increase efficiency, other increase area of coverage and accuracy. These techonologies have changed military needs, adding many more dimensions as well.

The Gulf War has initiated a search for weapons with greater utility, i.e., with discriminate effects, placing in background weapons of disutility, i.e., having indiscriminate effects, for example, cruise and stealth systems and precision munition. The aim is to cause as little damage to non-military assets and civilian poulation. The new technologies, called non-lethal technologies, like laser weapons, isotropic radiators, stem technologies, super caustics, etc., will open new vistas for civilian as well as military planners and the future 'spin-on' and 'spin-off' effects will profoundly alter the economic, political and military face of the country.

Non-Nuclear Technologies

The strategic thinking has been revolutionised by the arrival of non-nuclear technologies. In the field of military, a number of them has assumed significant roles, e.g., technologies relating to targeting, propulsion techniques, warhead efficiency, stealth technology,[20] space technology, missile technology and many others covered under 'key' and 'critical' technologies.[21]

Add to these above technologies, those which are concerned with never sophisticated communication systems, real time systems, telemetry, and non-lethal weapon technology. The whole array of new ultra sophisticated hi-tech environment of the 21st century opens up vistas whose absolute range and depth is unimaginable to-day. But whatever may be the future, Davies has rightly noted that one who would hesitate to readily accept the potential of technology and weapon application due to a habitual institutional resistance to fundamental changes would most likely be prevailed upon by a technologically inferior opponent because of willingness to be more innovative and to implement doctrinal changes.[22]

Conclusion

In the end, I submit that the Indian vision to have the best socio-cultural and politico-economic environment in the next millennium by having the best doctors, the best engineers, the best architects, the best scientists, the best bureaucrats, the best artists, etc., will come to naught if India does not also have the best, I repeat, the best, men and material to safeguard these best builders of our envisioned future India.[23] Ruskin opened his essay on "War" by noting that "War is a necessary evil". The author of Tarzan series, E.R. Burroughs, in one of his books, Tarzan and the Ant Men, explained how societies become licentious through a continuous peace. Human ingenuity can delay a war, can postpone it, but it can not be eliminated. There may not be a central war for years, but peripheral ones will rage, have raged, in the last five decades. Hence, during the long peace let us have the vision of Indian security upper-most in our mind to build an environment where peace and 'Good Life' can be sustained for a longer period than hitherto.

References

1. Howard Michael: Studies in War and Peace, Maurice Temple Smith, London, 1970, pp. 1-261.
2. Srivastava, H.K.: The India-Pakistan Strategic Debate, The Hold-Off Approach. Strategic Studies Journal, 1992, Vol. 5, No. 1 and 2, pp. 77-86.
3. Sl. No.1.
4. Srivastava, H.K.: India's Security in a Changing World. ISDA Journal, Vol. 1, No. 1, October-December 1991, pp. 44-51.
5. Ibid: Intransigent Pakistan and Indulgent India. IDR, Vol. 9(1), January 1994.
6. Singh, Jasjit: Security in a period of Strategic Uncertainty, Asian Strategic Review 1991-92 IDSA, pp. 7-26.
7. Knorr, Klaus: Limited Strategic War, in Limited Strategic War, ed. Knorr and Read, Thornton, Pall Mall Press, London, 1962, pp. 1-258.
8. Nye, Joseph., Jr.: The Transformation of World Power, The Amerian Review, vol. 34, No. 4, 1990, pp. 2-7.
9. Waltz, Kenneth N: The Emerging structure of Internatinal Politics. International Security Vol. 118 No. 2 (Fall) 1993, pp. 44-79.
10. Gorbachev, Mikhail: Speech to the Central Committee, May 1986.
11. Welch, Thomas, J.: Technology change and Security. The Washington Quarterly, Spring 1990, pp. 111-120.
12. Sing, Jasjit: The Challenge of Our Times, in India and the Nuclear Challenge, ed. K. Subrahmanyam, Lancer International, New Delhi, India, 1986. pp.15-50.

13. Brodie, Bernard: War and Politics, New York Macmillan, 1973.

14. Sl. No. 9.

15. List Frederick: National System of Political Economy. Quoted in Waltz.

16. "The School" refers to Adam Smith, David Ricardo and their followers.

17. Shinhara Miyohei: Industrial Growth, Trade, and Dynamic Pattern in the Japanese Economy. Tokyo,Tokyo University Press, 1982.

18. Sr. No. 9.

19. The Hindustan Times, March 14, 1994.

20. Davis, Jacquelyn K.: Technology and Strategy: Lessons and issues for the 1990s. ANNALS, AAPSS, 517, September 1991, pp. 203-216.

21. Srivastava, H.K.: Technologicaly-Dominant Strategic Future: The Potential of the India Service's Graduate IDRA, January 1993, pp. 42-50.

22. Sl. No. 20.

23. Adopted from a speech delivered by the author to the rotations of Pune in 1975 on the Teachers' Day.'

9

New Economic Policy and the Dwindling Role of Parliament in Indian Polity

R.K. Suresh Kumar *

The Background

The long-term impact of the 'Uruguay Round' will take some more time to be felt and judged since many of its provisions will only come into effect in a decade or so. To many in the country it is already a *bete noire*. For some others *a la* mode. The truth remains that the 'condottieri' who espouse its inevitability and need are not themselves convinced of its *raison d'etre*. The publication of the Asian Development Bank, the 'Asian Development outlook: 1993' notes:

> Prospects for the developing economies of Asia and the Pacific depend upon several factors including the pace of recovery in the world economy, maintenance of prudent macroeconomic policies and the ability to achieve and implement continued policy reforms and structural adjustments to maintain international competitiveness.[1]

The report in its concluding observation on Indian Economy further notes:

> The task of overhauling the policy framework is far from complete. The goverment still has to address some of the more difficult aspects of deregulation and structural change........ A similar degree of progress is not likely on all fronts ......, partly

* Senior Lecturer, Dept. of Politics Govt. Arts and Science College, Kozhikode [Calicut University]

> because of limits to the capacity to cope with rapid change, but also because of political pressure arising from social tensions caused for example, by rising unemployment of high inflation.[2]

Poverty reduction, which is a prominent objective of social and economic development in the Indian constitution, finds expression through plans and programmes aimed at providing more and more job opportunities. But the same report notes that:

> Prospects for employment are uncertain while the labour force is expected to grow at 2 per cent per annum, the on going structural reforms particularly technological upgrading and the development of a firm exit policy in industry and the public sector may check the emergence of sufficient employment opportunities, thus exacerbating the problem of underemployment and unemployment.[3]

Data from employment exchange registers indicate that the number of unemployed rose to 37.1 million during June 1992.[4] The above observations testify that the gerontocracy supervising the structural reforms are themselves in the position of a 'cicerone' not knowing its real worth.

Economic aspirations of the country and the Parliament's role

However the signing of the Dunkel Final Act by 117 nations including India on Dec. 15[5] has wide ranging ramifications for these countries. The sheer numerical importance of India in global demographic terms, makes our parliamentary democracy the most vibrating one.[6] In independent India, the list and content of legislations enacted by the parliament to benefit the disadvantaged sections of society remains quite impressive. The economic and social context prevailing in the country forced the framers of the constitution to include economic rights in the chapter on 'Directive Principles of State Policy'. The Right to quality, Right to Freedom, Right against exploitation—all these are envisaged as political rights in the constitution. Art. 21 which declares that no one can be deprived of his life or liberty without procedure in accordance with law also confers a political right. The person who is virtually denied liberty and full use of his life by economic exploitation doesn't come under its purview.[7] But our parliament has to its credit a number of impressive legislation to benefit the exploited like the contract Labour (Regulation and Prohibition) Act, '1970' The Bonded Labour

(Abolition) Act, 1976, The Inter-state Migrant Workman (Regulation of Employment and Conditions of Service)Act, 1979, The Child Labour (Regulation and Abolition) Act, 1986 and the like.[8] It was by taking the spirit of the constitution and not by following the word meaning that parliament enacted these bills and made amendments to the constitution relating to promotion of state sector, economic redistribution, land reforms, state's power to take over property, curbing economic exploitation and governmental initiative and control in public utility services.

Great strides were made in all these areas because of the implicit trust of the people in the initiatives of their representatives. These acts also enjoyed broad consensus of different sections of society. But the people of India now find themselves alienated from the decision making process of the country when the new national proprieties are being fixed conspicuously by scutling the parliament. The trust or consensus is also no more visible. The technocracy has become omnipresent and it is performing the functions that our parliament performed earlier quite competently. The distortion of our constitutionally committed objectives is being done by an elite who are not accountable to the people or to the parliament. They would allow the parliament only ceremonial eminence in our parliamentary form of government!

All this distortion seems to stem from the fact that those who subscribe to the photocopied model of 'Westminster democracy' believe that GATT is an international treaty and as such falls within the realm of executive power. They accept the parliaments power of scrutiny, not its power of sanction or veto. We have already seen how the Indian parliament read into the original text of the constitution and made amendments to the constitution benefiting the poor in India. These were not inroads into the constitution, but understanding and interpreting it in the then socio-economic milieu of the country which the parliamentarians were representing. In Britain, parliamentary government developed as part of experimentation in limiting and reducing irresponsible power whereas in India the ideas of representative government grew along with the national movement aiming at economic, social and political justice to the Indian people. So historically speaking, the parliament in the Indian context acquired original powers in the economic life of the nation.

The national movement implied movement not only to end colonial rule in India, but also to shape the economic destiny of the nation by uplifting the millions lying below the poverty line and by preventing economic exploitation of the weaker by the stronger. At the Lahore session of the Indian National Congress itself Nehru expressed his commitment to these ideals in the following words:

> I must frankly confer that I am a socialist and a republican and am no believer in kings and princes, or the order which .produce the modern kings of industry.[9]

The character of the 'New Condottieri'

> I an Roxborough, in his 'Theories of Underdevelopment' wrote: The choice of a growth model is not purely economic choice, made in a vacuum, it is made in a specific political and social context and entails specific social and political consequences.[10]

Unfortunately in India of today, western methods of production, western technology and western economic enterprises are all welcomed as important development agents. The historical experience of the country is not taken into account. Instead the 'Condottieri' of the ongoing economic reform process in the country are talking about the impracticality of applying value judgements to the process of modernization.[11]

The role of the parliament as was generally accepted for nearly three decades to bring about necessary economic changes in tune with the Indian reality stands minimised. The bureaucratic expertise venturing into parliamentary domains is questioning the very foundations of our cherished socio-economic goals which developed as part of the national movement for freedom. The point of worry is that the spurious substitutes offered under globalisation, which has tremendous impact on the poor masses of India comes from above, the parliament, the representative body of the Indian people regulated to the position of a mute victim. The bureaucratic decision makers understanding of modernity is surreptitiously packed with presuppositions of Western thinking which has no meaning to the vast majority of Indians. It would be apt here to quote from Mark Tully's latest book on India—wherein he writes :

> India is still a land dominated by foreign thinking ...... Colonialism teaches the native elite it creates to admire—all too often to ape—the ways of their foreign rulers. That habit of mind has survived in independent India.[12]

Sarcastically he adds :

> India's most successful students ...... now prefer Harvard or Yale. But what do they learn there which is relevant to the country? The scientists are versed in technologies aimed at reducing the role of human beings in production although labour is India's greatest asset. The doctors want to practice medicine which provides the latest and most expensive techniques of healing individuals, whereas India's need is for public health, preventive medicine and simple cures which can be administered by paramedical staff trained unexpensively. The business school graduates know how to administer complicated corporations with billion dollar assets—the sort of corporations which will put out of business the small, labour-intensive and unsophisticated industries that India is officially committed to encouraging.[13]

In the 1960s the neo-Marxist 'School of dependency and underdevelopment' challenged this type of modernisation concept. To them, the Third World was not a pre-modern world about to progress naturally to the level of the first.[14] India needs and escape form this section who have inherited the political and cultural biases of the colonial past. But this won't be an attractive alternative for these sections, because they would be the first casualties of such a step. This class knows very well that parliament is still a big enough influence in Indian polity and that it is better understood as an active partner in decision making process affecting the present and future generations. It is this role of the parliament that is being curtailed now as this has proved an unavoidable irritant for the government.

The Curtailment of Parliamentary Role

The parliament seems to be incapable of responding to the kinds of threats that comes from the votaries of globalisation. These votaries began their business in parliament with the script already half written. The re-reading of our national priorities—resulted in issuance of guidelines for the entry of new private sector banks and abolition of control over capital issues. Following recommendations of the Tax Reform Committee, a wide range of tax reforms was announced in the 1992 and 1993 budgets. Further reforms of trade and exchange rate policy were made in 1992 to strengthen the liberalization process and make trade policies more transparent. Export and import trade in selected goods which was previously reserved for government agencies, was opened up to private enterprise and exporters access to duty free imports was simplified. There was also a two stage liberalization of the exchange rate. First, the 1992 budget introduced a dual exchange rate system under which 40 per cent of foreign exchange earnings had to be converted at the official exchange rate and the balance at the market rate. Second, the rupee was made fully convertible on trade account with effect from the end of Feb. 1993. Policies towards foreign investment were also further liberalised during 1992 by permitting investment in previously reserved sections of the economy such as oil exploration and refining; widening the scope for investment by non-resident Indians, and treating companies with more than 40 per cent foreign equity the same as wholly Indian-owned companies.[15]

The government by authorising our negotiators to append their signatures to the GATT agreement, has actually given its assent.[16] The agreement violates our sovereignty by curtailing the power to decide policies not only in relation to foreign trade but in relation to such fundamental areas as agriculture, investment and social welfare. This amounts to mockery of people's sovereignty and parliamentary sovereignty.[17] The signing of the Dunkel Draft which affects the country's long term future, without taking parliament into confidence and evading a debate when parliament was in session meant the *coup de grace* to our avowed socio-economic goals.

The question remains whether a treaty of this magnitude which can change the character of our polity be signed sidelining the parliament? There is a view that the treaty will affect the legal system of the country. Some of the provisions of Dunkel Final Act affect Indian agriculture as well as health and well being of the people are subjects which fall under the jurisdiction of the states as per the Indian constitution. The Government of India doesn't have the constitutional authority to overlook this aspect without the prior concurrence of the constituent units of the federation. Likewise the new patent law under the would be WTO (World Trade Organisation) is against our legal system as it is the defendant country which has to prove its innocence in case of a complaint of injury.[18] The Government is also not prepared to constitute a JPC (Joint Parliamentary Committee) to discuss the provisions of the DFA. The change in the status of the government i.e., from a minority to a majority position in the Lok Sabha is also a matter of grave concern.

Mass discontent against this coup de grace is not being reflected inside parliament as a unified political force. There is no political party in India which has not condemned the present assault on our polity barring the ruling party. It is a known fact that many prominent members of the ruling party have strong reservations on the sidelining of the parliament. In spite of the above positive factors the parliament couldn't highlight the impact of the DDT (Dunkal Draft Text) on our agriculture. This has forced the farmers organisations like the KRSS (Karnataka Rajya Raitha Sangha) to take it to the streets by attacking the Bangalore office of the Cargill Inc; and the Cargill factory in Bellary. It was this act not the debates in parliament which opened up the present debate and forced the government to explain the true implications of the treaty signed on Dec: 15, 1993 in Geneva. Unless the parliament is able to bring governmental activities in this regard under open and critical scrutiny people's faith in our parliamentary system will erode. It is high time that the parliament stop playing the ceremonial idiot.

References

1. Asian Development Bank, *Asian Development Outlook—1993*, Oxford Uni. Press, (New York, April '93) See the Foreword-PIV.
2. *Ibid.*, p.144
3. *Ibid.*, p.143
4. *Ibid*, p.140
5. *Frontline* (Jan: 14, 1994), Vol.II. No.1, Report titled 'GATT: Little to cheer : India in the New Order', p. 36.
6. Around 16 per cent of the world's population lives in India. 5 million more births are occurring annually in India than in the People's Republic of China. The world Bank, *Population Change and Economic Development*, Oxford Uni. Press, (New York, 1985). Article by Tim Dyson: "An Assessment of Recent Demographic Trends in India".
7. Barbara Harris, S. Guhan and R.H. Cassen (ed.), *Poverty In India— Research and Policy*, Oxford Uni. Press, (Delhi, 1992). Article by Vasudha Dhagamwar: 'The Disadvantaged and the Law, p. 437.
8. *Ibid.*
9. B.N. Pande (Genl. ed.), *A Centenary History of the Indian National Congress (1885-1985)*, Vol. III, (N. Delhi, 1985) p. 220.
10. Ian Roxborough, *Theories of Underdevelopment*, Macmillan, (London, 1979, p-39.
11. R.T. Robertson, *The making of the modern world : An Introductory History*, Zed Books Ltd., (London, 1986) p. 147.
12. Mark Tully, *No Full Stops In India*, Penguin (N.Delhi, 1993), p. 3.

13. Based largely on the works of Paul Baran, Andre Gunder Frank, James Petras, Frantz Fanon, Samir Amin and Walter Rodney, the dependency school addressed itself directly to the failure of development strategies to achieve their goals.

    (R.T. Robertson, *Op. cit,* p. 147).

    This was necessary because the earlier school—the 'political development school'—underestimated the diversity among third world countries; the importance of political economy within nations and of the international economic order (James Manor (ed.), *Rethinking: Third World Politics*, Longman, (England, 1991), See the introduction—p. 1.)
14. Asian Development Bank, *Op. cit.,* p. 143.
15. *Frontline,* (Jan: 14, 1994), Vol .II. No. I Report titled: 'GATT: Little to Cheer: India in the new order,' p. 36.
16. *Ibid.,* see the editorial : 'Selling a surrender', p. 39.
17. *Economic and Political Weekly,* (Jan: 15 1994) Vol: XXIX, No. 3, Article by Arun Ghosh : 'GATT, MTO and the Indian constitution', pp. 77-78.

10

Tourism Marketing—A New Approach

K. Muraleedharan Menon

Tourism now enters into a new phase with exceptional demands and choices. As the tourists today are experienced travellers, they will not be satisfied with second rate attractions and amenities. It is a buyer's market. Hence there is demand for unique attractions and value for money. Invariably, it needs a careful marketing strategy.

The tourism has ceased to be a luxury reserved for a few at the top. Increased leisure and higher purchasing power have combined to enable more people to take part in tourism. Thus tourism is no longer the prerogative of the few. It becomes an accepted part of the life-styles of a number of people. Therefore, every country has a decisive role to play in tourism.

Every organisation, whether it is a Government Department, Public Sector or Private Enterprise, follows well defined objectives. Objectives in a free competitive market economy are different from those of a Centrally planned economy. In the same way, marketing objectives will change depending on the tourism policy of the country, its tourist products, its tourist organisation and management.

Tourism in the pure sense of the term is essentially a pleasure activity, in which money earned in one's normal domicile is spent in the places visited. It is thus a discretionary use of time and pleasure. The tourism has a hedonistic aspect that man is a pain-avoiding and pleasure-seeking animal who chooses the course of

* Post-Doctoral Fellow Dept of Politics, University of Kerala Trivandrum.

action that may maximise his pleasure. Tourist industry is based on the percepts that tourists will behave in ways that will bring them greatest pleasure. MacIntosh has affirmed this view, "perhaps upper-most of all individual travel motivation is simply the motivation for satisfying a person's need for pure pleasure".[1] The study on travel motivation is absolutely necessary for evolving a tourism marketing strategy. Professor Gray has postulated two main and distinct travel motivations: wander lust and sun lust.[2] The former refers to the seeking of locations containing better or different amenities to those available at home whereas the later refers to the experience of seeing new places, meeting new people and engaging in new and different activities.

In order to motivate a potential tourist to travel, a tourist image of the destination is required. The tourist image and motivation are related. For instance, in a political system where tourist image is on the decline, the tourist motivation for travel will also be negative. Again, a unique spot like the back waters of Kerala or Gulmarg resort of Kashmir if publicised properly, will motivate the potential tourists to visit the place. Therefore, the tourist motivation for a destination is depended upon the tourist image projected. The main task of the tourist organisation is to maintain the tourist image as orginial as possible and promote it as a unique attraction of the destination. The tourist product is an amalgamation of resources and created facilities of a destination.

The visitors are attracted to outstanding beauty which may be of a wide variety. In some areas it is the climate which is the major attraction, like mediterranean resorts, in some others, it is the mountain regions like Alps—"Water has always appealed as a source of relaxation whether it be associated with a sea-side beach, a waterfall or lake and river fishing".[3] Besides natural resources, people are attracted by the cultural heritage.

Tourism should be developed on the basis of the typology of the tourists. Since the taste of tourists differ widely proper attention must be given to the category of tourists and simultaneous promotion of tourism. There are different types of tourists who make different demands of a destination. The most important typologies of tourism proposed by the authors, Wahab, Cohen, Nolan, and Smith, are described below. Wahab proposed a five-fold classification based on the purpose of tourism. They are recreational tourism, cultural tourism, health tourism, sport tourism and conference tourism, Cohen divided tourists into four main types which recognize the individual motivation and experience.[5] They are the organised mass tourists, the individual mass tourists, the explorer and the drifter. This has been further divided into two types, Institutionalised and non-institutionalised. He grouped the first two into institutionalised and the last two into non-institutionalised. Nolan constructed a typology based on frequency and travel.[6] They are limited travellers, occasional travellers, regular travellers. Smith's typology is based on specific resons. They are recreational, cultural, historical, ethnic and environmental tourism.

No destination appeals to all tourists in the same way and the tourists may choose the destination for more than one reason. Again, the demands also vary according to the demands placed by the different types of tourism on the destination area. Therefore, the government must evolve a suitable marketing strategy for attracting different types of tourists.

The marketing of tourism is a widespread phenomenon but the methods of marketing have received little attention from either tourism planners or researchers. The British Insitute of Marketing defined marketing, "as the management function which organizes and directs all those business activities involved in assessing and converting customer purchasing power into effective demand for a specific product of service and in moving the product or service to the final customer or user so as to achieve the profit target of other objectives set by the company."[8] The American Management Association defines marketing as "the identification or creation of customer needs and then the motivation and co-ordinated use of all functions within a business that can fill these needs with benefit to buyer and seller."[9] Even though marketing is a function of management, these definitions focus on customer rather than the product. According to Philip Kotler, marketing means human activity that takes place in relation to markets.[10] Again, he demarcates two concepts: the selling concept and the marketing comcept. The selling concept starts with the company's existing products and calls for heavy selling and promotion to achieve profitable sales. The marketing concept, on the other hand, starts with the company's target customers and their needs and wants, the company integrates and co-ordinates all the activities that will affect customer satisfaction and the company achieves its profit through creating and maintaining customer satisfaction.[11]

Thus the classical concept of marketing was to sell the goods and services produced and it would include all activities that aim at bringing the product to the consumer. The concept, therefore was production oriented, promotion and selling to achieve and end x which is profit through sales volume. The new concept of marketing therefore, deeparts from the premise that production should start with the needs of the consumer.[12]

Old Concept :	Production →	Sales	→	Consumption
New Concept :	Consumption →	Integrated	→	Production
	←	Marketing	←	

The classical concept of profit making through sales volume is changed to a concept of consumer satisfaction which in its turn results in enhancing the sales volume.

Present concept in National Tourist Organisation (NTO)	Tourist product →	Promotion and sales through various outlets. →	Return through Tourist volume increase.
New Concept	Touriest as customer. → ←	Integrated marketing → ←	Return through tourist satisfaction.

Peter Druckar is right when he felt that "there is only one valid definition of business purpose: to create customer". He further argues ".....because its purpose is to create the customer, the business enterprise has two basic functions: marketing and innovation."[13]

Tourism is qualitatively different from other industries. Tourism is a service, production and consumption all of which take place, at the same time. It is one of few industries in which the consumer actually collects the service personally from the place where it is produced.[14] Tourism product can neither be transported to the customer nor can it be stored. A manufactured product, say, a bottle of soft drink, can be sold on some other day, if it is not sold on a particular day. But, if airline seats, hotel rooms, etc. are not sold today, certainly they are lost for ever. Another distinguishing feature of tourism from other industries is that tourism supply is relatively fixed. Hence there sources and infrastucture of a destination cannot change as quickly as can tourist demand.[15] On the other hand, demand for tourist service is unstable. That is why the seasonal variations, political disturbances, epidmic, currency fluctuations, etc. have affected tourism. Another feature that makes tourism different from other industries, is that the service provided—a vacation is infact, an amalgam of several products and services.[16] For example, transportation, lodging, food beverage, etc. are the different elements of a vacation and these are usually supplied by different firms. Since each individual firm provides only a part of the final product, tourism sector requires a high degree of specialisation and co-operation. The tourist product covers the complete experience from the time the tourist leaves home to the time he returns.

An analysis of the tourist products is an essential requisite for tourism development. According to Kotlar, marketing's short-term task may be to adjust customer's wants to existing goods, but its long-run task is to adjust the goods to customer's wants.[17] Hence, it is important to carry out a detailed investigation of the potential market, to prepare a detailed inventory of the state resources, to chart cost-benefit analysis, to identify consumer habits and attitudes, etc. for the healthy development of tourism. Therefore, tourism marketing means systematic and co-ordinated execution of business policy to achieve the optional satisfaction of the needs of identifiable consumer groups and to achieve an appropriate return. In fact, the method of marketing has changed from the concept of profit-making through an increased sales volume, to consumer satisfaction.

A considerable volume of research has taken place in the field of tourism. Usually, as it has been done by the private agencies such as Airlines, tour operators, etc., the results derived by them cannot be made available. This has slowed down further research. Furthermore, the difficulty in collecting the accurate statistics has complicated the market research in tourism.

The Primary function of the tourism organisation is to derive two questions: (a) how can total market be increased? (b) how can a country obtain the maximum share of that market? Thus the main task of the marketing research is to supply the basic information such as the current size of market, the types of visitors, whether the market is changing, how can a country sell its products for maximum profitability, etc.

Some of these informations can be obtained by analysing statistical data while others by specific surveys. Different categories of survey are identified by the International Union of Official Tourism

Organisations (IUOTO) (Hand book DII).[18] They are: overall comprehensive survey, survey of existing domestic and/or future tourist demands, survey limited to exit or entry points, survey during transportation, survey in the main destinations, survey in the main selling points.

Market surveys can be conducted in the country of origin of the main tourist flow and in a number of potential market areas. In order to assess the trends of tourist flow, the researchers must take into account of the changing patterns of tourists. Very few destinations attract only one category of tourist. It is a general fact that the tourists are of many kinds. Hence, a thorough classification is required to identify various groups or flows. Many of the groups have quite different characteristics. They may need different facilities. In order to measure the overall socio-economic influence and trends the main tourist group have to be studied individually. The study of each tourist group may benefit to determinate (a) its volume, seasonal fluctuations and trends (b) its socio-economic characteristics, professions, ages, etc. (c) its motivations (d) its consumption characteristics, duration of stay, level of spending, etc.

The tourism involves movement of people in pursuit of the tourist product. Every tourist has his own reasons to visit a particular destination. Hence, the individualistic nature of tourists whether travelling alone or in groups may have a demand which should be studied properly with a view to develop a marketing technique. Other factors which affect the marketing technique should also be examined clearly :

a. Political factor

Tourism movement may be sensitive in the tourist generating countries when these countries are affected by political tensions and clashes. Also the tourist movement will come to an end if the diplomatic relations among the tourist generating countries and tourist receiving countries become strained.

b. Administrative factor

If rigid frontier and travel formalities are imposed by the destination country on the tourists, it may affect the tourist flow.

c. Cultural factor

Cultural factor also has a profound influence on tourism. The travel is more prevalent in cultured societies. The likes and dislikes of the tourists may also differ from one country to another.

d. Economic factor

The economic stability of a country has to be studied. The tourism, in a strict sense of the word, is very much depended on the spending habits of the tourists.

In fact, the countries which adopt the best marketing techniques, will get the best opportunity to improve their economy. The reliable tools of marketing research are field work and Desk research. The main functions of the former are collection of reliable records of tourist flow which include the country of residence, the length of stay, expenditure pattern, motivation and preferences. The latter analyses the available statistics of tourists and the published information on tourist markets. The international bodies like UNESCO, WTO, OECD, IATA, etc., publish reliable data which are of very useful in analysing statistics. The communication methods are very effective in tourism marketing. To create awareness of the products to the consumer is the main function of the marketing technique. These are made possible through sales promotion and information services. The former aims at persuading the potential tourists to visit the destination. The service of the tour operators and travel agents can be used for this purpose. The main activities of the sales promotion are: advertisements, publicity distribution, direct mail, exhibitions, trade fairs, film shows, etc. The farmiliarisation tour, organised for the tour operators, travel writers, etc., is another indirect method of sales promotion. The information services, on the other hand, aim at providing practical advice and information to the tourists for arranging their tour programmes and accommodation facilities in the destination countries. The activities of the information services are public enquiry regarding customs, climate, food, clothing, hotel lists, tariffs, local transportation, places of interests, etc. Thus marketing research is a continuous process aiming at gathering information for evolving a new marketing strategy.

The travel trade expands rapidly. Almost all the countries in the world have good prospects of expanding their tourism business.

The urge to travel to remotest regions will flourish. New attractions, amenities and resorts are being developed throughout the world. The countries all over the world are competing to secure a share of this cake. In short, those countries which adopt the best marketing techniques, have every possibility of getting the best chance of increasing their share of the tourism market.

References

1. Robinson. H: A Geography of Tourism, Macdonald and Evans Ltd. Great Britain, 1976. 29.
2. Mathiesan and Wall. G: *Tourism—Economic,Physical and Social* Impacts, Longman, English, 1984, 31.
3. Murphy. P.E: Tourism—*A Community's Approach,* Methuan, New York, 1985-13.
4. Wahab. S: *Tourism Management,* Tourism International Press, London, 1975, 10.
5. Noronha Raymond: *Social and Cultural Dimensions of Tourism,* World Bank staff working paper No. 326, 1979, 2.
6. Noronha Raymond.
7. Wahab. S.
8. Wahab, L.J. Crampon and L.M. Rothfield: Tourism Marketing, Tourism International Press, London, 1976. 21.
9. Wahab, L.J. Crampon and L.M. Rothfield, 21.
10. Kotlar Philip: *Principles of marketing,* Prentice Hall, New Delhi, 1985, 13.
11. Kotler., 18.
12. Wahab., 102.
13. Drucker Pater. Management: Task responsibilities, Practices-61.
14. Peters Michael: *International Tourism,* Hutchinson & Co. Ltd, London, 1969.
15. Robert Christie Mill and Alastair Morrison: The Tourism system—An introductory Text, Prentice Hall, New Jersy, 1985, 357.
16. Robert Christie Mill and Alastair Morrison.
17. Kotler. P: *Marketing Management—Analysis, Planning, Control.* Eugle Wood Cliffs, New Jersey, 1967.
18. Lawson Fred and Band-Bovy Manual, Tourism and Recreation Development, CBI Publishing Co, USA, 222.

11

The Union Budget—1995-96 A Critical View

K. Ramachandran Nair *

The Union Minister of Finance, Dr. Manmohan Singh, the chief architect of India's Economic Reforms since 1991, succeeded in presenting his fifth consecutive budget. The budget was described as populist and voter friendly. Some believe that the budget influences the voter, but now it also seems true that the voter influences the budget. In the case of the Union Budget for 1995-96, the Finance Minister has tried to see the *"human face"* which was totally ignored in the earlier four budgets. What are the intentions of Dr. Singh? How far are they going to be materialised? If not, where will they lead the country to? This paper is an attempt to take a critical view of the Union Budget for 1995-96 which was presented to the Parliament on the Ides of March this year. First we take a look at the Economic Survey for 1994-95 which represents the backdrop to the budget for 1995-96 and then we go to examine the specific claims the Finance Minister has made. This is followed by an analysis of the critical fiscal parameters and conclude with some comments on the post-budget developments like the amendments made to the Exim Policy.

Economic Survey—1994-95

Let us look at the Economic Survery for 1994-95. It warned against indulging in "fiscal populism", even as it conceded that the fundamental objective of the economic reforms should be to bring

* (Dr. K. Ramachandran Nair, Professor and Head, Deptt. of Economics, University of Kerala).

about a sustained improvement in the living standards of people. It pointed out that the cost of fiscal populism could be extraordinarily high and long-lasting. It identified areas which require further attention. They included liberalisation of consumer goods imports, wide-ranging changes in unnecessary legal and bureaucratic impediments, freeing consumer electronics and agro industries from licensing controls, removal of price and distribution controls on Petroleum products and coal and cut in wasteful expenditure of the government. In short, the survey wants greater reforms. But what have reforms brought to the country and its people so far?

The survey indicates an upswing in the economy during 1994-95 including a growth rate of GDP at 5.3 per cent. This is, however, followed by a warning. It says: "undeniable achievements are not free from threat". This was particularly so because in "today's increasingly open and competitive international environment, perceptions of weaknesses in macro economic policy or economic reforms could easily affect adversely the flow of foreign savings". The data part of the survey is largely a repetition of the RBI Report on Currency and Finance, 1993-94. While the survey presents a winsome portrait of the economy, it does not just ignore the dangers of a 11 per cent inflation. There are also more than subtle indications in the survery about the imperatives surrounding the *"human face"* in the budgetary process and the protection of the weakest and poorest sections of society. It is clear from the above that even after the presentation of four budgets by the reform architect, Dr. Singh, the basic weaknesses of the Indian Economy have not changed any bit. However, based on the survery, the Finance Minister has made certain specific claims. We would like to examine how far are these claims true and valid.

The Claims

Dr. Singh in his budget speech said thus: "Four years have passed since our government under the leadership of Prime Minister, Shri P.V. Narasimha Rao, took office in the midst of an unprecedented economic crisis. Our immediate task was to save the nation from a relentless slide into the abyss of falling production, soaring inflation and deepening poverty. We dealt swiftly with the immediate crisis and we also worked towards a broader objective of shifting the economy on to a path of rapid employment generating growth. Our aim was to raise India to her rightful place in the comity of nations". Of course the serious crisis that emerged to the surface in July 1991 was managed through some emergency measures like sale/ pledge of gold (both monetary and non-monetary), the devaluation of the Rupee (described officially as a mere exchange rate correction) and a feeble attempt at fiscal consolidation. It is analogous to what doctors do when a seriously ill patient is brought to the Emergency/ Casualty ward in a hospital. And once the conditions stabilise, further concrete work in nursing the patient back to good health has to be undertaken. What the Economic Survey tells us that even the proposed stabilisation has not been done, Consequently, most of the fiscal parameters continue to be unstable thereby causing anxiety even among the supporters of India's economic reforms.

GDP Growth

As against the GDP growth of 3.8 per cent in 1993-94, India was able to achieve a higher rate of growth in 1994-95, of about 5.3 per cent. Past experience suggests that higher rate of growth of GDP does not ensure jobs for millions of unemployed. This is supported by declining trend in employment elasticity. The GDP may have grown even if goods and services for satisfying basic human needs are not produced. The composition of output suggests that after 1991 there has been a significant shift in favour of production of "white goods". Production is targeted to satisfy elitist consumption and the process behind it is always capital intensive. No wonder, people now speak about *"jobless growth"* which is going to be a distinguishing feature of the post-reform economy.

The year 1994-95 witnessed a 3 per cent growth in agricultural production, foodgrains out-put reaching a record high at 185 million tons. But as everybody knows economic reforms were not responsible for this good performance of agricultural sector. It were indeed good mansoons that caused it. The Finance Minister also claims that the higher procurement in 1994-95 led to a high buffer stock of 31 million tons. But despite this, food prices have been rising in 1994-95. The offtake of foodgrains from the Public Distribution System also registered a declining trend. One wonders why the issue prices under the PDS rose to a level closer to open market prices rather than the latter coming down to the level of PDS prices. In a country where a large proportion of population is below the poverty line and many are suffering from under malnutrition, the buffer stock was not found used to tackle this problem nor was it used for controlling inflation.

Employment

The Finance Minister claims that "growth has created new jobs for our people. In 1991-92 total employment grew only by 3 millions. In each of the two years thereafter, employment increased twice as fast, with about 6 million new jobs added each year. The increase is expected to be even higher in 1994-95. The drawing room Cassandras, who predicted massive unemployment as a consequence of the reforms, have been conclusively proved wrong". This claim has to be compared with the government's own Eighth Plan target of 8.2 million. If new employment generation is not neutralised by loss of employment to the already employed, there may be a net gain. The government has not given any data on loss of employment consequent on implementing economic reforms. In another part of his budget speech the Finance Minster says: "Experience in our own country, as also from all over the world, shows that the surest antidote to poverty is rapid and broad-based growth." Given the close interrelation between the level of employment and level of poverty in India, as well as given the low employment elasticity the economy has exhibited so far, it becomes clear that generation of more employment and thereby reduction of the level of poverty in India will greatly depend on how fast the economy grows. In this context the crucial question is whether even the 5 plus growth rate is sustainable? If we look at the major sources of this growth rate, we would find that it is largely a demand-led growth, where demand has been artificially stimulated by public expenditure, fiscal deficit and inflow of FOREX. The broad parameters of the budget for 1995-96 show that public expenditure is going to be curtailed drastically to achieve some sort of fiscal stability. In 1990-91 capital expenditure was 6 per cent of total expenditure. It steadily came down to reach 4.3 per cent in 1994-95 and is expected to go down further to 3.4 per cent. It may also be seen that growth has been largely confined to non-commodity sectors.

Trade Gap

The Finance Minister claims that "liberalisation and openness have actually increased our self-reliance. Exports now finance over 90 per cent of imports, compared to only about 60 per cent in the latter half of the eighties. The external deficit on current account (CAD) was over 3 per cent of GDP in 1990-91. It is expected to be less than 0.5 per cent in 1994-95". It is true that in 1991-92 the dollar value of India's exports fell by 1.5 per cent. For this, part of the blame should be put on global market conditions. It increased by 3.8 per-cent in 1992-93 and further by 19.6 per cent in 1993-94, but declined to a lower rate of increase of 17.3 per cent in 1994-95. Imports on the other hand recorded an increase of 10.8 per cent in 1991-92, 32.4 per cent in 1992-93, 14.9 per cent in 1993-94 and 23.6 per cent in 1994-95 in rupee terms. This is a reflection of changes in the external value of the Rupee. But one thing is clear, that in 1994-95 in rupee terms exports were only of Rs. 65483 crores as against imports of Rs. 71248 crores, thus giving a trade gap. The so-called *"remarkable turn around"* mentioned by Dr. Manmohan Singh did not help to reduce the trade gap even after four years of reforms". Though exports have registered an upswing, thanks to the depreciating Rupee, the exporters are not keen in bringing their foreign exchange earnings to India because they expect the Rupee to depreciate further. The deregulation in the foreign exchange market has helped the exporters in this matter. A recent study by the Confederation of Indian Industry (CII) has shown that many exporters are keen in selling their exportable goods in the domestic market rather than taking the risk in competitive selling in the global market. The exporters, as every one knows, constitute a class pampered by the government with subsidies, tax concessions and other benefits and it is this class which now freely engages itself in such actions which normally deprive the nation of valuable foreign exchange. Exporters' lobby and their political clout seem to continue even after the economic reforms were initiated.

The problem of widening CAD cannot be ruled out now since signing the GATT Treaty. With the emergence of World Trade Organisation (WTO) India's exports are going to be hit much harder. The recent controversy on imposing social clauses or conditions will restrict India's exports further. At the same time due to import liberalisation, India's imports are likely to increase substantially. The net result would be larger CAD. In terms of as a proportion of GDP, the CAD in 1994-95 may be only 0.5 per cent. But in absolute terms as compared to 415 million dollars of CAD in 1993-94, the CAD in 1994-95 was about 1000 million dollars. This is not a remarkable achievement.

The FOREX

In his budget speech Dr. Singh spoke about the remarkable turn around in FOREX. "They had fallen to barely one billion dollars in June 1991. On March 10, 1995 (five days before the 1995-96 budget was presented) they stood at over 20 billion dollars". It is true that FOREX has increased remarkably, but what is its composition? Broadly speaking, the most important components of the FOREX are the funds brought in by NRI, Foreign Institutional Investors (FII) and by foreign companies. Of these, the last, also known as Foreign Direct Investment (FDI), has been the least. Even there, the cost of these funds has been on the high side especially when contrary to the advice of the World Bank, the Government of India started giving counter-guarantees to foreign companies like ENRON. A recent report produced by the IDBI has stated that after a few years the ENRON company, a big US multinational, would be reaping a net rate of return in the range of 16 to 40 per cent. The report also points out a trick played by these MNCs in padding up their investment cost. After a few years India will have to find foreign exchange to clear the expatriation of funds by these companies.

One important inplication of the mounting FOREX is on the growth of money stock M3. For every dollar that flows into India, technically speaking the RBI has to create equivalent rupees at the given exchange rate. But when more dollars come, the prevailing exchange rate cannot be maintained as the rupee will start appreciating. An appreciating rupee is not liked by exporters as it will reduce their rupee earnings against dollars derived from exports. In this context the RBI decided to sterilise the dollars so as to keep the dollar-rupee rate stable or in other words to keep the rupee depreciated as it exists now. But in this sterilisation exercise the RBI incurred an exchange loss of nearly Rs. 500 crores because it had to borrow to buy the dollars.

The massive FOREX inflow and their efficient management became an issue in debate. Suggestions have been made regarding how to reduce the FOREX. They included (a) liberalisation of imports of commodities including consumer items, (b) keeping GDR subscriptions/funds mobilised in Europe, in Europe itself and bringing them into India only when the borrowing company really needs funds, (c) prepay past high cost liabilities, etc. Any way the FOREX increase is creating problems in macro economic management.

External Dept

Close on the heels of the claim on FOREX, the Finance Minister said: "At the time of the crisis, our external debt was rising at the rate of 8 billion dollars a year. In 1993-94 the increase in external debt was reduced to less than one billion dollars. In the first half of 1994-95, our external debt stock actually declined by almost 300 million dollars". Instead of smaller increase in the stock of external debt, one should now start worrying about the total stock of external debt which in 1994-95 reached 90 billion dollars. This involves an annual interest liability of 10 billion dollars. Our exports cannot earn enough dollars to meet interest liability on past debt. Then how are we going to pay interest as well as repay a part of the principal of the loan? As we do with our internal liabilities, one may say that we will borrow and repay. This indeed is bad management. It is also seen that since reforms were initiated in 1991, the proportion share of short-term debt as compared to that of long-term debt has declined sub-stantially. This implies that Dr. Singh is trying to defer the burden of external debt to a distant future. In that case the cost of servicing the debt also becomes large.

Fiscal Situation

Since the IMF-World Bank started advising India on designing an economic reform programme, the concept of fiscal deficit became a popular one. A look at the budget for 1995-96 suggests a total neglect of fiscal consolidation and stability.

Union Budgets at a Glance

(Rs. Crores)

	1993-94 Actuals	*1994-95 Budget Estimate*	*1994-95 Revised Estimate*	*1995-96 Budget Estimate*
1. Revenue Receipts	75453	86084	88770	10078
2. Capital Receipts	55440	59615	67502	66364
3. Total Receipts	130893	145699	156272	167151
4. Revenue Expenditure	108169	118811	122902	136328
5. Capital Expenditure	33684	32888	39370	35823
6. Total Expenditure	141853	151699	162272	172151
7. Revenue Deficit (1-4)	32716	32727	34132	35541
8. Budgetary Deficit (3-6)	10960	6000	6000	5000
9. Fiscal Deficit [(1+Recovery of Loans+ Other receipts)—6]	60257	54915	61035	57634
10. Primary Deficit	23562	8915	17035	5634

According to fiscal literature the following concepts of deficits need to be distinguished:

(a) Revenue Deficit = Revenue Receipts-Revenue Expenditure

(b) Budget Deficit = Total Receipts-Total Expenditure

(c) Fiscal Deficit = (Revenue Receipts + Recoveries of loan + other receipts)-(total expenditure)

It can also be calculated as the sum of borrowings and other liabilities of the Government of India and Budgetary deficit.

It may be seen that the budget deficit in 1995-96 is kept at Rs. 5000 crores as against Rs. 6000 crores in 1994-95. But fiscal deficit in 1995-96 is put at Rs. 57634 crores since along with budget deficit of Rs. 5000 crores one has to add Rs. 52634 crores as borrowings and other liabilities. In other words, of all the concepts of deficits, the most crucial ones are the fiscal deficit and the revenue deficit. In India, both these have shown dangerous trends.

For instance, the size of revenue deficit is a sign of financial profligacy and indiscipline of the government. The revenue deficit in 1995-96 was Rs. 35541 crores as compared to Rs. 32716 crores in 1993-94. On the other hand fiscal deficit in 1994-95 as per revised estimate was larger than that in 1993-94 actuals. In 1995-96 the fiscal deficit is marginally less. If we deduct interest payments from fiscal deficit, we get Primary Deficit. There is always wide variation between budget estimate and revised estimate, but this is more patent in the case of primary deficit. In 1994-95 budget estimate, the primary deficit was only Rs. 8915 crores, but it became Rs. 17035 crores, nearly double in the revised estimate. It is likely to go up further when the actual accounts are finalised. The same is the case of fiscal deficit as well as revenue deficit.

The IMF World Bank advice given to India in 1991 was that India should bring down its fiscal deficit from 8.7 per cent of GDP to 5 per cent within five years. India failed in this exercise. To say that the fiscal deficit has only gone up to 6.75 per cent of the GDP as against the target of 6 per cent is not much of a consolation given the fact that the GDP itself has swollen by an inflation rate of over 11 per cent. If the revenue deficit and the fiscal deficit are to shoot beyond the levels projected, the country may have to live with double-digit inflation once again with, prospects of continuing it for a longer period, because fiscal deficit may affect inflation and infla tion may affect fiscal deficit. According to the Finance Minister the fiscal deficit in 1995-96 will be 5.5 per cent of GDP and he says "I would have liked to do better, but on balance I feel that a fiscal deficit of this order can be absorbed if the existing growth momentum is maintained." It is indeed interesting to note that for almost every claim made by the Finance Minister he is clever enough to put forth a few assumptions and "ifs".

How is he planning to keep down the fiscal deficit? Before we answer this, let us take a look at what Bhagwati and Srinivasan suggested in their monograph *India's Economic Reforms* (July 1993). They drew the attention to the following areas of concern and remedial action in the context of large fiscal deficit (i) The reductions in developmental expenditure to keep down the fiscal deficit could create difficulties down the road, (ii) there is further scope for cuts in non-developmental expenditure especially in regard to the emoluments and size of the bureaucracy and subsidies to public sector enterpises and to agriculture, (iii) there is need to raise mere revenue by expanding the tax base, (iv) a sound management of monetary policy in the interest of financial stability requires that the financial sector reforms be implemented at greater speed.

It is found that Dr. Manmohan Singh threw these pieces of advice to the winds with his budget for 1995-96. First, he cut developmental expenditure. Plan expenditure in 1994-95 was Rs. 48761 crores and this was cut to Rs. 48, 500 crores and given the inflation rate, it is considerably less in real terms. Second, he increased non-developmental expenditure.The non-plan expenditure was increased from Rs.113510 crores in 1994-95 to Rs. 123650 crores. Subsidies have been raised. Third, he did not make any attempt to broaden the tax base. Instead, he announced cuts in Union excise and customs on the assumption that at the reduced tax rates, revenue buoyancy will pick up. Fourth, no sound monetary policy or speeding up of financial sector reforms has been promised. Instead, commercial banks have been asked to bear the burden of financing new anti-poverty programmes. Banking industry felt that it was let-down. The financial sector reform indeed got derailed. The finance minister broke the continuity to financial sector reform.

A comparison between capital receipts and capital expenditure is very revealing. In 1994-95 the Government of India's capital receipts amounted to Rs. 67502 crores. Of this the amount set apart for capital expenditure was only Rs. 39370 crores leaving a surplus of Rs.28132 crores in the capital account. In 1995-96 the capital receipts and capital expenditure would be Rs 66364 crores and Rs. 35823 crores respectively leaving a surplus of Rs. 30543 crores which is larger than that of 1994-95. The surplus in the capital account has been used for reducing the deficit in the revenue account. Despite this adjustment the revenue deficit in 1995-96 is projected at Rs. 35541 crores as compared to Rs. 34132 crores in 1994-95.

Another way for reducing fiscal deficit is raising more revenue by broadening the fiscal base and making the structure of taxes efficient. The Chelliah Committee has made the necessary proposals for this, but the Union Finance Minister has not attempted anything substantial in this direction. At the same time he has proposed to raise a few thousands of crores of rupees by way of disinvestment of PSU equity. The sale of equity is exclusively meant to reduce the fiscal deficit and to some extent retire part of high cost debt.

A major component of non-development expenditure in India now is interest payments. We have reached a stage when the purpose of fresh borrowing is not making capital expenditure but pay interest on outstanding liabilities. In 1992-93 the Union government's net borrowing came to Rs. 27861 crores and interest payments amounted to Rs. 31035 crores. In 1994-95 it borrowed Rs. 48915 crores and paid Rs. 46000 crores (budget estimate) as interest payments on past liabilities. The internal liabilities in 1980-90 constituted 52.5 per cent of GDP. It increased to 54.8 per cent in 1993-94 but it is projected to decline to 51.6 per cent by 1995-96. But this is more than overshadowed by the increase in interest payments from 3.9 per cent of GDP in 1989-90 to 4.8 percent in 1994-95 and 5 per cent in 1995-96.

The Union Minister of Finance and the RBI reached an agreement on the modalities of government borrowing with a view at infuse a certain amount of fiscal discipline in managing government borrowing. One important component of this agreement is that hereafter the government would borrow much of its required funds from the open market rather than from the RBI. This has three major implications. First, the cost of government borrowing would go up substantially as open market rates of interest are invariably higher than the low rates changed by the RBI. Second, when government enters the funds market and compete with non-government borrowers, the latter would be crowded out and they would have to seek other sources. Third, the competition between government and non-government borrowers would naturally push up the lending rates due to overall shortages. This might even induce the RBI to adopt an expansionary policy leading to the accentuation of the existing level of inflation.

Another thing that worries us is the continuation of fiscal imbalance despite the buoyancy in government revenues. Revenue receipts in 1993-94 stood at Rs. 75453 crores. It increased to Rs. 88770 crores in 1994-95 as per the revised estimates as against Rs. 86084 crores given in the budget estimates. According to the budget estimate for 1995-96 revenue receipts are projected to reach an all-time high of Rs. 100780 crores. The decomposition of revenue receipts into the tax revenue (net to centre) and non-tax revenue, it is found that the increase in tax revenue was substantial from Rs. 53449 crores in 1993-94 (RE) to Rs. 64988 crores in 1994-95 (RE). The projection for 1995-96 is Rs. 74374 crores. The non-tax revenue increased from Rs. 22004 crores in 1993-94 (RE) to just Rs.23782 crores in 1994-95 (RE) and it is expected to increase only to Rs. 26413 crores in 1995-96 (RE). This suggests that the governments should tap the non-tax revenue much more vigorously.

Inflation Control

In his budget speech the Union Finance Minister said thus: "Inflation has surfaced again as a serious problem. We had succeeded in lowering the rate of inflation from the peak of 17 per cent in 1991 to around 7 per cent in the middle of 1993, but since then, inflation has accelerated again and currently exceeds 11 per cent. This acceleration has occurred because of several factors. One reason is the sharp increase in procurement prices in the previous three years. Another is the shortfall in production in critical sectors such as sugar, cotton and oilseeds. The persistence of fiscal deficits at levels higher than they should be has also contributed to inflationary pressures. Recognising these problems, we will tackle inflation on a priority basis in the year ahead." A closer analysis of facts would show that the government would fail in controlling inflation.

The government has failed in containing the fiscal deficit as well as revenue deficit within manageable levels. Both of them are still very large. While the government has cut down plan expenditure from Rs. 48761 crores in 1994-95 to Rs. 48500 crores in 1995-96 (the latter if adjusted for current inflation rate would be substantially lower) the non-plan expenditure increased from Rs. 113510 crores in 1994-95 to Rs. 123650 crores in 1995-96. The monetisation of fiscal deficit as well as the FOREX inflows would only accentuate the pace of inflation. Besides the government has not till now abandoned its policy on administered prices. Despite comfortable FOREX position, the government has not started seriously thinking about using the FOREX to import sugar, cotton and oilseeds, particularly edible oils to ease supply shortages. The all-round cuts in excise duties were expected to bring down the commodity prices but that did not happen yet because the producers refuse to pass on the benefits to consumers. An upset in the monsoon may make the situation serious. The buffer stocks are not being used to bring down open market prices of foodgrains. The monetary policy has not been tightened adequately to control inflation. All this shows that government's claim on controlling inflation would not materialise.

Attack on Poverty

The Finance Minister claims that his 1995-96 budget would step up the attack on poverty. He said thus: "In my first budget speech itself, I have emphasised that economic growth and restructuring are not ends in themselves. They are only the means to improving the lives of ordinary citizens. I wish to assure the House that this concern has been central to our strategy from the very beginning. Experience in our own country, as also from all over the world, shows that the surest antidote to poverty is rapid and broad-based growth.This is precisely what our economic reforms seek to achieve". But the Finance Minister seems to ignore that a 5-6 per cent rate of growth is inadequate to remove poverty in India and if this growth is narrow-based by focussing on commodities that are consumed by the elites, growth would never act as an antidote to poverty.

The Finance Minister seems to be a believer in the trickle-down mechanism because he said: "We also recognise that the fruits of growth will take time to reach some of the poorest and weakest sections of our society" assuming that at least some would reach the moderately poor. To ensure that even the poorest and the weakest receive the benefit in the short run, he gives the highest priority to strengthening programmes of rural development, employment generation, primary education, primary health and other key social sector programmes. He would prefer to continue with the two-track strategy of accelerating growth, investment and modernisation on the one track and strengthening anti-poverty programmes on the other.

The Finance Minister then proposed a few eye-catching populist schemes: (1) To encourage quicker completion of projects in rural infrastructure a Rural Infrastructural Development Fund within the NABARD from April 1995 will be set up. This will create a corpus of Rs. 2000 crores for completion of rural infrastructure projects. (2) In the one hundred predominantly tribal districts, NABARD will open an exclusive line of credit to Co-operatives and Regional Rural Banks for meeting the credit needs of scheduled tribes. Rs. 400 crores have been earmarked for this in the budget for 1995-96. (3) NABARD is to earmark another Rs. 100 crores for financing SC/ST beneficiaries in both farm and non-farm activities. (4) The banks are to provide Rs. 1000 crores on a consortium basis to the Khadi and Village Industries Commission (KVIC) to be lent to viable Khadi and Village Industry units and this will be guaranteed by the government. (5) The NABARD is to be directed to extend refinancing to commercial banks also (besides District and State Corporative Banks) for extending credit to Coperative handloom institutions. (6) A Technology Development and Modernisation Fund is to be established in the Small Industries Development Bank of India (SIDBI) to provide financial assistance to quality projects aimed at strengthening export capability of small scale industries. This fund will have Rs. 200 crores. (7) Extension of the National Equity Fund Scheme started in 1987 to all tiny small scale units irrespective of their location except for units in metropolitan areas. The scope of this scheme is to be expanded to cover expansion, modernisation, technology upgradation and diversification. (8) A new North Eastern Development Bank (NEDB) is going to be established to finance creation, expansion and modernisation of industrial enterprises and infrastructure projects in the region, the constituency of the Finance Minister. The NEDB will have an authorised capital of Rs. 5000 crores with initial contributions coming from all-India financial institutions like the IDBI, ICICI and UTI. (9) The Indira Awas Yojana (IAY) will be used to build 50 lakh rural dwelling units in the next five years. (10) To softer the hardship of the old and the weak, a National Social Assistance Scheme (NSAS) is proposed. One component of the scheme is the provision of a national minimum old-age pension of Rs. 75 per month of people above 65 years of age and who are below the poverty line. A second component is expected to provide lumpsum survivor benefits of Rs. 5000 to poor house-hold on the death of the primary bread winner. The third component aims at the provision of sustenance for pre-natal and post-natal maternity care to women belonging to poor households for the first two births. The scheme will eventually cover about 14 million neediest beneficiaries from households below the poverty line. Three quarters of the beneficiaries are likely to be women needing assistance on account of old age, widowhood and maternity. The scheme, according to the Finance Minister, is to be funded jointly by the Centre and the states but will be implemented by the states through Panchayati Raj institutions. (11) The social assistance package is to be complemented by a new group Life Insurance Scheme of the LIC and to be implemented by the Panchayats in rural areas. A life cover of Rs. 5000 will be provided for a modest annual premium of around Rs. 70. For poor households, the Centre will subsidise 25 per cent of the premium with the states meeting an equal amount and the beneficiary contributing 50 per cent. The subsidy will be limited to one policy per poor household. For others there will be no subsidy on the premium. According to the Finance Minister, the main object of the scheme is massive promotion of social assistance and thrift in rural areas with the active involvement of the Panchayats. For the poor house-holds, this is expected to act as a second tier of partly subsidised security supplementing the survivor benefits and will inculcate the habit of saving (12) The Central government is to participate in the phased expansion of the mid-day meals scheme and for this a Committee will be set up to work out the modalities.

The above dozen schemes are treated as new initiatives for funding agricultural infrastructure, promoting Handlooms and Khadi and Village Industries, expanding rural housing and introducing social assistance/insurance. They are expected to strengthen the anti-poverty component of the strategy which will go along with the on-going economic reforms. A close look at the programmes suggests that the Centre proposes them, but the burden of implementing them will be on the states, Panchayat Raj institutions and institutions like the NABARD, IDBI, ICICI, UTI and the LIC. It is also seen that as the centre's share of the money needed to implement the programmes, the Budget for 1995-96 makes no extra provision. The question is where is the money? Do states possess additional resources particularly after the Report of the Tenth Finance Commission? This Report recommends drastic cuts in plan and non-plan transfers to states with serious implications for federal polity. The Centre's Welfare Schemes are going to put severe strains on the banks giving the impression that financial sector reforms are getting fast derailed contrary to the views of the Narasimham Committee Report on the subject. An impression is also created that what the Union Budget for 1995-96 has indicated is only a set of financial targets. In order to implement the social assistance schemes about 13 new agencies have to be set up and several committees have to be appointed to work out the modalities.

The Centre's priorities as reflected in the overall budgetary allocations suggest a tragic distortion. For drinking water supply the budget provision for 1995-96 is Rs. 700 crores as against Rs. 460 crores in 1994-95. But this is the amount needed to buy two jet passenger aircrafts. Between the passenger aircraft or drinking water supply which is the most important priority? The former of course gets the priority in the scheme of things in the present-day India. Despite the IRDP, NREP, TRYSEM, JRY and other anti-poverty programmes, poverty continues to be a big problem and it is a simple question to ask, how are the new dozen schemes going to resolve the problem of poverty. The old-age pension of Rs. 75 per month means Rs. 2.50 per day and contributes little to help the beneficiary. The trickle down possibilities are also questioned.

Middle Class Bias

Every budget possesses a bias tilting in favour of a particular social/economic class and as such the budget for 1995-96 seems to possess a clear bias in favour of the middle class. The Finance Minister has raised the basic income tax exemption limit to Rs. 40,000, taking a large number of tax-payers out of the tax net. This is followed by substantial cuts in custom duties of such goods as printed circuits, colour T.V. sets, computer, integrated circuits, hard disks, and LPG, While the change in the income tax limit create a loss of Rs. 1582 crores, that in the customs create a loss of Rs. 1179 crores. The reductions in the customs are expected to hit the grey market (black/smuggled market) very badly. The duty relief on LPG is meant to help the private companies who have been permitted to import bulk quantities of LPG. This is to be viewed against the rapid expansion of parallel marketing of LPG in India today.

The budget proposal on the TD's interest in operationally impractical since the banks oppose it and the depositors may try to escape the tax liability by fractioning their deposits and putting them in different accounts and banks. One must not forget that already benami deposits create problems in controlling black money.

Tax reforms continue in the Union Budget for 1995-96 too to some extent. This is evident from the emerging long-term trend in the ratio of direct taxes to indirect taxes. In 1980-85 it was 27 per cent and by 1994-95 it reached 40 per cent. The Budget, in a sense, has brought about some amount of stability in the tax structure. But one demand of the private corporate sector was not accepted by the Finance Minister. The surcharge on Indian companies was not abolished while foreign companies are exempted from this. The idea of providing level playing field is thus put in cold storage.

Amended Exim Policy

It was in 1992 that the Union government declared the new Exim Policy for a period of five years. This policy was an integral part of india's economic reforms. In support of this policy Bhagwati and Srinivasan made out a strong case for greater liberalisation of imports. According to them, in India tariffs are still high and non-uniform. While on average, consumer goods imports are constrained by Quantitative Restrictions (QRs), capital goods and intermediate goods imports are constrained by tariffs. Tariffs have a predominantly revenue generating effect rather than a resource-allocating effect in the consumer goods sector whereas they have a significant resource-allocating effect in the capital and intermediate goods sectors. India's tariff structure, according to Bhagwati and Srinivasan, has a bias against consumer goods. Available data clearly show that the rates of duties on consumer goods are the highest, while the rates on capital goods are the least. This is supported by the Chelliah Committee too. The effective rate of protection (ERP) in India always exceeded nominal rate of protection (NRP). There is also a discrepancy between the official duty rates and the collection rates. With QRs liberalised and import tariff coming down from highly restrictive levels, one may expect the volume response to liberalisation to be large and, therefore, it is argued that customs revenues may not come down.

The tariff structure, despite the new Exim Policy of 1992, continued to be characterised by a multiplicity of rates-advalorem and specific duties. The Chelliah Committee, the Alexander Committee and the Long Term Fiscal Policy document had recommended for greater simplification of tariff structure. Bhagwati and Srinivasan pleaded for greater liberalisation of consumer goods imports by abolishing the so-called *"sin taxes"* meant to discourage import of luxuries. The idea that the removal of consumer goods imports restrictions will lower the savings rate is, according to them, fallacious. "Luxuries" of 1950s and 1960s are no longer luxuries in the 1990s particularly for the growing middle class. Some of these goods, like personal computers, may be productive. Restricting import of luxuries may stimulate production of similar import substitutes. Further these restrictions may induce a shift of demand from such imports to demestically produced non-tradeables. The fears that liberalisation of imports through reduction of duties may reduce government revenues may also be not true. Here the Laffer Curve is advanced to justify tariff cuts.

The government introduced in October 1992, the Special Import Licences (SIL) to ease up a little on consumer goods imports. The SILs permitted a small single-digit fraction of the export earnings by certain classes of exporters to be used to import consumer goods on the positive list of restricted consumer goods imports. These imports fetched a premium. The scheme utilised the scarcity permium on consumer goods imports to subsidise exports. In the Indian system we used to have besides the SILs, the OGL, Restricted List, Negative List,etc., for regulating imports and save on FOREX. Now FOREX being large, the government compelled further by its commitments under the GATT Treaty, decided to go in for a major amendment to its 1992 Exim Policy. When Chidambaram was reappointed as the Commerce Minister in the Union Cabinet, it became clear to everybody that this strong votary of economic reforms will surely go for further liberalisation of imports. This became true with the amended Exim Policy of 1995.

Let us see the main features of this policy. To help domestic producers capital goods imports valued up to Rs. 20 crores can be imported without duty. The export earnings will, hereafter, be outside the control of the RBI as well as Exim Policy. Goods received as gifts can also be imported free of duty. Hereafter components, spare parts and all kinds of consumer durables will be treated as consumer goods. The OGL list was expanded substantially by including even such items as gum, audio tapes, children's napkins, clinical thermometers, dried fish, nail cutters, particle boards made from saw dust, paper, sewing needles, coffee, milk powder, sports goods like shuttle cock, hockey stick and football, surgical gloves, quartz-analogue watches, computer floppies, etc. The SIL list is also expanded to include colour TV, picture tubes, computers valued up to Rs. 1.5 lakh, diesel generating sets of up to 1500 KV, cash and accounting registers, refrigerators and deep freezers used for commercial purposes, safe deposit lockers, cash boxes, ceramic products used in laboratories, tube lights and halogen lights, pins, paper clips, staplers, writing instruments, bull dozers, motorised sewing machines, telecom equipments, vitamin B-12, etc. One wonders why most of these goods already being produced in India, some particularly in the small-scale sector, should be allowed to be imported liberally. India already exports some of these goods. What is then the main objective of the new Exim Policy? The zero duty import of capital goods is expected to give substantial benefit to the MNCs like Daewo, Mercedes-Benz, Volkswagan, Ford, Hyuandai, Fia, etc., who are now eyeing the Indian market for their cars. If the domestic companies including the Indian affiliates of these MNCs have no export obligation, the Exim Policy is going to give them substanital gains.

Hotels and tourist promotion agencies can now import luxury foreign cars at low tariff. Even our national carrier, the Indian Arilines, is permitted to import foreign liquor, toilet paper and seat covers from abroad liberally. Services have been equated with commodities and as a result liberalisation of imports has been extended to cover financial and banking services, hotels, advertisement agencies, computer software companies, law firms, etc. The Negative List has been cut short substantially and only three commodities have been completely banned from imports. Electronic goods have been taken out from the Negative List. The liberal import of milk powder is going to hit the National Dairy Development Board (NDDB) very badly. It may be remembered that India is one of the largest producers of dairy products in the world, second only to the USA, and the NDDB, is an outcome of the Operation Flood which strengthened the movement of milk producers' co-operatives and brought about a big socio-economic revolution in the countryside.

Where are we being led to ?

Where are the economic reforms and their instrumentalities

like the Budget and the Exim Policy going to lead us to? Are we deliberately breaking the backbone of indigenous industry and sacrificing self-reliance? Are we opening up our domestic markets to global sellers? Are we going to push up Indian prices to the global level? There appeared recently in the national dailies an advertisement issued by the Indian Oil Corporation saying that *"Indian Oil is proud to welcome MOBIL back to India"*. The SHELL insignia/motto has already appeared and the walls of petrol bunks run by Hindustan Petroleum Company. The ONGC has decided to lease out to the MNCs its productive oil fields for exploitation. It should be noted that the ONGC has already spent several crores of rupees in exploring for productive oil fields and it is such oil fields that have proved their potential that are being leased out for a song. The disinvestment of PSU equity has been going on in violation of the guidelines given by the Rangarajan Committee and this money has not been spent either for reinvestment in the PSU or for creating additional jobs. Public assets built over the years with public money have been sold to help the government to reduce its fiscal deficits. The Social Safety Net and the National Renewal Fund have not taken off despite the World Bank assistance given to India. The picture is not as rosy as the Union Finance Minister describes. One cannot forget that the Indian Economy was very open when the East India Company came. After four decades of independence and pursuit of self-reliance, we are again opening up the economy to finance capital as compared to industrial and merchant capital during the colonial rule.

Conclusion

Though the main thrust of this paper was on the Union Budget 1995-96, we could not just ignore the overall economic policy scenario and their implications. However in conclusion, we shall confine our remarks to the Union Budget. The Union Budget for 1995-96, we believe, does nothing to raise the domestic saving and investment ratios and capital formation in the country. It has failed to maintain or raise the level of plan/public investment. It has failed to contain the financial profligacy of the government despite its intentions to reduce the role of the government. Both revenue deficit and fiscal deficit have continued to be vulnerably high. Government's failure to contain inflation is also clear from the budget parameters. The states are going to get less funds while they are being burdened with new responsibilities. The budget has no plan to check hot money flows. The schemes to help the poor may not take off for want of adequate provision of funds in the budget. On the whole Dr. Manmohan's fifth budget is not going to take the country any further towards the goal of growth, stability and equity.

References

Economic Survey 1994-95.

Union Budget—1995-96.

J. Bhagwati and T.N. Srinivasan: *India's Economic Reforms,* July, 1993.

Vijay Joshi and I.M.D. Little: *India: Macroeconomics and Political Economy, 1964-1991.* Oxford University Press, 1993.

Deepak Nayyar: "Indian Economy at the Cross-roads Illusions and Realities", *Economic and Political Weekly,* April 10, 1993.

Manu Shroff: "Indian Economy at the Crosswads" *Economic and Political Weekly,* May 8, 1993.

Sanjaya Baru: "New Economic Policy: Efficiency Equity and Fiscal Stabilisation". *Economic and Political Weekly,* April 10, 1993.

Economic Times, (Various issues).

Financial Express (do.)

Main Stream (do.)

12

India's Exports and Imports Problems and Prospects

*N. Niyathi**

International trade barriers are slowly narrowing down and a new era of world trade is emerging. In the newly emerging global economy export and import trade will play a major role since inter dependence between economics on several aspects is increasing. But interdependence on trade and developoment aid between countries is viewed with caution by most developing aid between countries is viewed with caution by most development countries as they believe that developed countries are always motivated to sustain their interests and under such situation, interests of developing countries may get partly neglected. It is because of this fear that most developing countries first hesitated to sign the Dunkel report on trade. India being a developing country has to protect its national interests of development and therefore export-import trade policy has to be designed and implemented accordingly. India's foreign trade policy has been followed by controls and regulations on import and export with a view to protect domestic industry and trade. In order to protect domestic industry and trade from foreign goods high import duty has been levied on imported goods and again imports were regulated and controled through licence and import substitution production measures. Despite all the controls and regulations and import substitution measures India's foreign trade deficit has been increasing and it reached at alarming heights during late 1980s when India resorted to large-scale borrowing from international financial institutions to settle trade deficit crisis.

* State Planning Board, Thiruvanan Thapuram.

In 1980-81, India's export was valued at Rs. 6711 crores and import at Rs. 12549 crores which ended in a trade deficit of Rs. 5838 crores. Export increased to Rs.10895 crore and import to Rs. 19658 crore in 1985-86 ending in a deficit of Rs. 8763 crore. Trade deficit further increased to Rs.10635 crore in 1990-91. India experienced unprecedented foreign exchange reserve crisis in 1991 when India's foreign currency reserve fell down to below one billion dollars which was only for two weeks import payment. In order to overcome the 'foreign money crisis' trade reforms were started in 1991 which are being continued. It so happened not because of huge foreign trade deficit alone but also because of huge foreign debt service payments. For example, during 1985-86 to 1990-91, import increased by only 120 per cent against 199 per cent export increase. During 1990-91, ratio of debt service payments to current receipts was 32.3 per cent as against 10.2 per cent in 1980-81 and 18.7 in 1985-86. Between 1990-91 and 1994-95, export increased by 101 per cent when import increased by only 65 per cent. In 1991-92, initial year of trade reforms, 92 per cent of import payments were met through export earnings. Table 1 below shows absolute value of export and import and the trade deficit. It shows that trade deficit which was Rs. 10635 crore in 1990-91 had been brought down to less than one-third to Rs. 3259 crore in 1993-94. But provisional figures indicate that during 1994-95 trade deficit has again increased to Rs. 5755 crores.

Table 1 : Value of Exports and Imports from India

(Rs. Crore)

Year	*Exports*	*Imports*	*Trade Deficit*
1980-81	6711	12549	5838
1985-86	10895	19658	8763
1990-91	32558	43193	10635
1991-92	44041	47851	3810
1992-93	53688	63375	9687
1993-94	69547	72806	3259
1994-95 (April-Jry)	65483	71248	5755

Our policy-makers believe that with reduction on duty on import Indian products are supposed to become internationally competitive in quality and cost effectiveness. In the past import duty was liked and retained at higher level to protect Indian made domestic porducts in the market. Continued protected market system did not help Indian industries to develop competitiveness in quality and cost. Import-substitution export-import policy followed since independence has partially hindered technology upgradation and blocked productivity increase and cost reduction. Basic industries reserved in the public sector not only became inefficient but also loss making white elephants, eating public money. In the private sector as well, most of the domestic industries failed to develop cost effective suitable technology to improve efficiency and productivity. Therefore in the new reform policy, import of both capital goods and consumer goods are allowed to make Indian industries more cost effective with suitable technology upgradation either through import or through internal improvement. In the present setup, with the arrival of Multi National Corporations with modern cost effective technology and quality control, can Indian domestic industries sustain and expand without foreign help and aid. This, in fact, is a vital issue which needs long standing remedial measures insted of short living measures. Annual change in export-import policy or reduction in import duty are only short-term remedial measures. Improvement in productivity through cost-efective and quality control measures together with emport incentives and relaxation of export-import rules and procedures should constitute the ultimate aim of our foreign trade policy. Only under such a condition that India can attain sustained growth in exports and sustained decrease in imports.

India's export-import trade gathered significant momentum since economic reforms started in July 1991 when foreign trade shifted from control to open market. This, in fact, facilitated structural change in export trade. In 1980-81 ratio of export to import was 52.4 per cent. In other words, only 52 per cent imports payments were met through export earnings. The export-import ratio had been only 66 per cent in 1990-91. But after the decontrol of foreign trade in 1991-92, export grew at a higher rate than import which resulted in decline in foreign trade deficit. The ratio of export to import increased to 86.7 per cent in 1991-92 and further to 94.6 per cent in 1993-94. In other words, nearly 95 per cent of India's import payments were earned through exports in 1993-94 as against 66 per cent in 1990-91. It is against an export coverage ratio of only 52 per cent in 1980-81 which caused to huge trade deficit. Reform led improvement in export-import trade together with better invisible account mainly resulted to a sharp reduction in the current account deficit from 3.3 per cent of GDP in 1990-91 to 1.8 per cent in 1992-93 and still down to 0.1 per cent in 1993-94. Similarly debt service payment also decreased from 32.3 per cent of current receipts in 1990-91 to 24.8 per cent in 1993-94. Indian economy has thus attained stable and sustainable balance of payment position since the trade reforms started in July 1991. Table 2 below shows the major indicators of a stable balance of payment position of India.

Table 2 : India's Balance of Payment—key Indicators

Sl. No.	*Indicators*	*Years* 1980-81	1985-86	1989-90	1990-91	1991-92	1992-93	1993-94
1	2	3	4	5	6	7	8	9
1.	Ratio of Export to Import (per cent)	52.4	54.7	69.5	66.2	86.7	81.2	94.6
2.	Current account deficit to GDP (per cent)	1.6	2.3	2.0	3.3	0.4	1.8	0.1
3.	Ratio of Debt service payments to current receipts (per cent)	10.2	18.7	31.8	32.3	29.8	30.3	24.8
4.	Ratio of trade deficit to GDP (per cent)	4.5	3.7	2.5	2.2	0.7	1.5	0.5

Commodity-wise Emports

In our export primary products and manufactured products form the major share. Major items under primary products are marine products, tea, coffee, cotton, cashew kernel and tobacco and among manufactured products major items are gems and jewellery, engineering goods, chemicals, textiles and readymade garmets. Export of marine products in value terms almost increased by five times between 1980-81 and 1990-91. Between 1985-86 and 1993-94, increase was by six times. Export value of coffee and tea more than doubled from Rs. 640 crore in 1980-81 to Rs. 1304 crore in 1990-91 and reached the level of Rs. 1553 crore in 1993-94. Export value of three major items, namely, fish, vegetables & fruits and coffee and tea together formed 16 percent of export in 1980-81 but reduced to nearly nine per cent in 1990-91 and further down to six per cent in 1993-94. Value of manufactured goods exported which was only Rs. 2320 crore in 1980-81 increased by nearly eight times to Rs. 17391 crore in 1990-91 and further increased to Rs. 31404 crore in 1993-94 forming nearly 53 per cent of India's total export. Within the manufactured products handicrafts, engineering goods and readymade garments formed the major share in value terms in 1990-91. Handicrafts has been the single largest manufactured product exported from India and its export has been increasing rapidly since trade reforms in 1991. In 1992-93 value of handicrafts export increased by 31 per cent and in 1993-94 increase has been 36 per cent. Export of readymade garments which showed 28 per cent increase in 1992-93 showed only 17 per cent increase in 1993-94. It is against a total increase in exports by 22 per cent in 1992-93 and 30 per cent in 1993-94. Export of rice increased by 29 per cent in 1992-93 and 31 per cent in 1993-94 against 64 per cent increase in 1990-91. Total agriculture and allied products exported in 1992-93 increased by 15 per cent and by 38 per cent in 1993-94. Manufactured products which together constitute nearly three-fourth of our exports showed 25 per cent increase in 1991-92 and 28 per cent increase in 1992-93 against 39 per cent increase in 1990-91. Export of primary and manufactured products have achieved higher rate of export growth before trade reforms started in 1991 which indicate that India has more export potential for these products in the coming years. Table 3 shows growth in the product-wise export since 1980-81.

Table 3 : Commodity-wise Export from India

Commodities	*Years*				
	1980-81	*1985-86*	*1990-91*	*1992-93*	*1993-94*
1. Food Items	1077	1714	2924	3096	4508
	(16.1)	(15.7)	(8.9)	(5.8)	(6.5)
(i) Marine products	217	420	960	1743	2537
(ii) Vegetables & Fruits	220	403	660	312	418
(iii) Coffee & Tea	640	891	1304	1353	1553
2. Beverages and Tobacco	141	171	296	474	461
	(2.1)	(1.6)	(0.9)	(0.9)	(0.7)
3. Petroleum Products	25	645	938	1379	1248
	(0.4)	(5.9)	(2.9)	(2.6)	(1.8)
4. Chemicals & related products	235	394	2345	3669	4650
	(3.5)	(3.6)	(7.2)	(6.8)	(6.7)
5. Manufactured goods	2320	3711	17391	28562	31404
	(34.5)	(34.1)	(53.5)	(53.1)	(45.0)
6. Machinery Transport and Equipments	526	704	2428	7023	1840
	(7.8)	(6.5)	(7.5)	(13.1)	(2.6)
7. Others	2387	3556	6231	9485	25630
	(35.6)	(32.6)	(19.1)	(17.7)	(36.7)
Total	6711	10895	32553	53688	69751
	(100)	(100)	(100)	(100)	(100)

(Figures in bracket indicate percentage to total)

Commodity-wise Imports

Despite annual increase in trade deficit India's import has been increasing. Between 1980-81 and 1990-91, India's import increased by 3.4 times from Rs. 12549 crore to Rs. 43193 crore. Similarly increase in import was 3.2 times from Rs. 19658 crore in 1985-86 to Rs. 73101 crore in 1993-94. Between 1990-91 and 1993-94, our import almost doubled from Rs. 43193 crore to Rs. 73101 crore. In our import POL stand first followed by capital goods and manufactured goods. However the share of POL in total import has been decreasing rapidly in recent years as a result of increase in its domestic production. In 1980-81, out of the total import, POL shared nearly 42 per cent and after one decade in 1990-91, its share decreased to 25 per cent. However in 1993-94 POL is estimated to share 27 per cent of India's import. Value of POL import more than doubled between 1980-81 and 1990-91. Between 1990-91 and 1993-94, import of POL increased by only 66 per cent. Import of capital goods on the other hand increased by nearly four times during 1980-81 to 1990-91 and almost doubled between 1990-91 and 1993-94. Since the trade reforms in 1991, July, import of capital goods is showing an increasing trend consequent on reduction in its import duty to a low level of 35 per cent to 45 per cent in 1994-95 and further down to 25 per cent in 1995-96. Machinery and capital goods are vital for industry and as a result of reduction of import duty on capital goods, its import has increased. Industry has responded well to this new policy and has attained 25 per cent growth on capital goods industry during April-November 1994. Table 4 below shows India's commodity-wise import since 1980-81.

Table 4 : Commodity-wise Import to India

Commodities	*1980-81*	*1985-86*	*1990-91*	*1992-93*	*1993-94*
1. Food Items	380	878	173	966	266
	(3.0)	(4.5)			
2. Petroleum	5263	4989	10816	17142	18055
products	(41.9)	(25.4)	(25.1)	(27.0)	
3. Vegetable oils	683	749	326	167	164
	(5.5)	(3.8)	(0.8)	(0.3)	-
4. Chemicals and	1325	2873	5447	8104	
related products	(10.6)	(14.6)	(12.6)	(12.8)	-
5. Manufactured	2153	3580	8138	17424	-
products	(17.2)	(18.2)	(18.8)	(27.5)	18944
6. Capital goods	1910	4285	10465	8811	
	(15.2)	(21.8)	(24.2)	(13.9)	

7. Others	835 (6.6)	2304 (11.7)	8001 (18.5)	10761 (17.0)	35672
Total	12549 (100)	19658 (100)	43193 (100)	63375 (100)	73101 (100)

(Figures in bracket indicate Percentage to total).

Direction of Foreign Trade

In India's total foreign trade (export plus import) share o. OECD countries and developing countries together formed 63 per cent in 1980-81, 75 per cent after a decade in 1990-91 and 78.8 per cent in 1993-94. While India's trade share with OECD countries do not show stable growth, trade share with developing countries show a stable growth. For instance, share of trade with developing countries increased from 17 per cent in 1980-81 to 21 per cent in 1992-93 and to 22.4 per cent in 1993-94 share of OECD countries decreased from 58 per cent in 1992-93 to 56.4 per cent in 1993-94. Trade share with Eastern Europe has been decreasing rapidly from 15 per cent in 1980-81 to 12 per cent in 1990-91 to 3.4 per cent in 1992-93 and again to 3.3 per cent in 1993-94. Increasing trade share with developing countries is a good indication in the sense that India can still increase trade with these group of countries even in the long run because with rapid economic growth, their demand for food and manufactured products will increase. Table 5 below shows India's trade share with major group of countries. It shows that after the collapse of the former Soviet Union and consequent change in Eastern Europe, India's export to these countries has come down.

Table 5 : Share of each Zone in Total Foreign Trade

(Rs. crores)

	1980-81	*Per-cent*	*1990-91*	*Per-cent*	*1992-93*	*Per-cent*	*1993-94*	*Per-cent*
1. OECD Countries	8873	46.1	43101	56.9	68001	58.1	80525	56.4
2. OPEC Countries	4235	21.9	8872	11.7	19014	16.2	23804	16.1
3. Eastern Europe	2862	14.9	9192	12.1	3968	3.4	4704	3.3
4. Developing Countries	3237	16.8	13616	18.0	24668	21.1	31968	22.4
5. Others	53	0.3	961	1.3	1414	1.2	1851	1.3
Total	19260	100	75746	100	117063	100	142852	100

Direction of Export

Out of total export from India, share of OECD countries is not only more but also increase continuously. In 1980-81, out of India's total export 46.5 per cent was with OECD countries and the share increased to 56.5 per cent in 1990-91 and to 60.5 per cent in 1992-93. But it marginally decreased to 55.9 per cent in 1993-94. Share of export with OPEC countries on the other hand has been decreasing gradually from 11 per cent to 5.6 per cent in 1990-91 and again increased to 9.6 per cent in 1992-93 and to 10.6 per cent in 1993-94. The share of Eastern Europe decreased substantially from 23 per cent in 1980-81 to 17.9 per cent in 1990-91 and to 4.4 per cent in 1992-93 and to 4.5 per cent in 1993-94. Meanwhile share of export with developing countries has been gradually and continuously increasing as shown in Table 6 below. For instance, the share of exports increased from 18.8 per cent in 1980-81 to 23 per cent in 1992-93 and improved further to 26 per cent in 1993-94. Thus in India's export trade, the share of OECD and developing countries together form about 80 per cent in recent years (See Table)

Table 6 : Groupwise Export and its Share

(Rs. crores)

Group	*Years*			
	1980-81	*1990-91*	*1992-93*	*1993-94*
1. PECD Countries	3126	18389	32466	39670
	(46.5)	(56.5)	(60.5)	(55.9)
2. ODEC Countries	745	1831	5180	7441
	(11.1)	(5.6)	(9.6)	(10.6)
3. Eastern Europe	1521	5819	2359	3038
	(22.8)	(17.9)	(4.4)	(4.5)
4. Developing	1266	5560	12269	18114
	(18.8)	(17.1)	(22.9)	(26.0)
5. Others	53	954	1414	1488
	(0.8)	(2.9)	(2.6)	(2.0)
Total	6711	32553	53688	69751
	(100)	(100)	(100)	(100)

Direction of Imports

In import as well, share of OECD countries are more but the share is decreasing in recent years. Similarly import share from East European Countries also show decreasing trend. However, share with developing countries is increasing marginally. For instance, in 1980-81, out of India's total import, OECD share was nearly 46 per cent and it increased to 57 per cent in 1990-91 but decreased to 56 per cent in 1992-93 and 1993-94. Meanwhile import share with OPEC countries which stood at 27.8 per cent in 1980-81 decreased to 16 per cent in 1990-91 and increased to nearly 22 per cent in 1992-93 and 1993-94. The share of Eastern Europe substantially decreased from 10.7 per cent in 1980-81 to 7.8 per cent in 1990-91 and further down to 2.5 per cent in 1992-93 and 2.3 per cent in 1993-94. Share of developing countries in India's import decreased from 16 per cent in 1980-81 to 19 per cent in 1990-91 and 1993-94 (See Table-7). All these show that in India's export and import trade, the share of OECD and developing countries are substantially higher.

Table 7 : Group-wise Import and its Share

Group	*1980-81*	*1990-91*	*1992-93*	*1993-94*
1. OECD	5747	24712	35535	40855
	(45.8)	(57.2)	(56.1)	(55.8)
2. OPEC	3490	7041	13834	16363
	(27.8)	(16.3)	(21.8)	(22.4)
3. Eastern Europe	1341	3377	1609	1666
	(10.7)	(7.8)	(2.5)	(2.3)
4. Developing Countries	1971	8056	12399	13854
	(15.7)	(18.7)	(19.6)	(19.0)
Others	-	-	-	363
				(0.5)
Total	12549	43193	63375	73101
	(100)	(100)	(100)	(100)

Note: Figures in bracket indicate percentage to total.

India's export items have not undergone any significant change since the trade reforms except marginal variations. Manufactured products formed 78 per cent of India's total export in 1994-95 as against 76 per cent in 1993-94. Within manufactured products two items, namely gems & jewellery and readymade garments formed 17.4 per cent and 11.4 per cent respectively. Cotton yarn and fabrics formed 8.6 per cent and leather goods formed 4 per cent. In other words these four products together forms nearly 45 per cent of total goods exported from India in 1993-94. Among the export of commodities manufactured goods has shown the highest increase in 1994-95 over 1993-94. Within manufactured goods cotton yarn showed 41 per cent increase and electronic goods showed 25 per cent increase. Agriculture products which formed nearly 16 per cent of total export in 1994-95 increased only marginally. Export of raw cotton decreased by 81 per cent, unmanufactured tobacco by 44 per cent and cereals by 17 per cent. Export of coffee increased by 208 per cent. Collapse of the former Soviet Union and disturbed conditions in Russian markets have adversely affected the export of manufactured products to that country.

Trade reforms initiated since July 1991 as part of economic reforms relaxed administrative controls to induct flexibility in export. The intention has been to liberalise the tightly controlled and complex trade regime with nominal tariffs, qualitative restriction on import and export and import substitution through manufacture. As part of it, exchange value of rupee was devalued twice during 1991-92 by 22 per cent. Again, convertability was allowed to Indian rupee, first partial convertability and later full convertability on current trade account. Under partial convertability authorised dealers have to surrender 40 per cent of foreign currencies at the official exchange rate fixed by RBI and 60 per cent of foreign currency earned were allowed to be sold at market rate. The procedure for capital goods import was simplified and exporters were allowed to open foreign currency accounts in approved banks. In March 1992, a new Export-Import Policy was announced as part of the economic reforms for the 8th Plan period 1992-97 which eliminated licensing, quantitative restrictions and regulatory control. Under the new policy export and import were allowed except the regulation by negative lists of export and import. List of export were reduced to 79 items. In the negative lists export and import items were reduced to 79 each. Again in 1992. September, import items in the negative lists were further decreased. In order to ensure internationally accepted standards of quality for export products manufactures and exporters were made eligible for special import licence. The new policy also allowed selective duty-free import required for the purpose of export production subject to fulfilment of a time-bound export obligation. These changes were affected to increase export and to earn more foreign currency to strengthen our foreign currency reserves.

The trade reforms have to be viewed with respect to the already announced EXIM Policy for the eighth Plan 1992-97 and its achievement untill 1994-95. During the 7th plan trade deficit had been 2.7 per cent of GDP. In the 8th Plan,, export import policy, the target is to reduce the trade deficit to 1.6 per cent of GDP and to increase the exports annually at 13.6 per cent and import at 8.4 per cent in volume. Moreover in the total exports from India the share of manufactured products are targeted to form 76 per cent. The share of export in GDP is proposed to be raised to 9.6 per cent during the 8th Plan. The target envisaged for the 8th plan is already under achievement. For instance trade deficit to GDP has been brought down to 0.7 per cent in 1992-93, 1.5 per cent in 1993-94 and 0.5 per cent in 1994-95. In 1993-94, share of manufactured products in our total annual exports has been 75 per cent. In 1992-93 the share had been 76 per cent. In 1994-95, the provisional figures show that manufactured products form nearly 78 per cent which is above the 8th Plan target of 76 per cent. India's recent export-import trend indicates several favourable factors which would promote to stabilise the exchange value of Indian rupee.

Trade reforms have contained the growth of import as compared to export which resulted to a decline in trade deficit. In 1991-92, first year of reforms, value of import increased at 10.8 per cent as against an increase of 35 per cent in export. In dollar terms import and export decreased by 19 per cent and 1.5 per cent respectively. In 1992-93, second year of reforms, while import increased by 32 per cent export increased by only 22 per cent. In the third year, trend again changed in favour of export when it increased by 30 per cent against the import increase of 15 per cent. In 1994-95, the provisional figures indicate that imports have increased by 7 per cent more than the export increase of 17 per cent. The trend after trade reforms thus indicate that export and import neither increase nor decrease on a sustained level to suitably stabilise the foreign trade. So long as such foreign trade stabilisation are impossible to attain, it will become difficult to ensure and attain the foreign trade target envisaged in the 1992-97 Exim policy. This can be achieved only if export growth is accelerated and import growth is decelerated with the liberalised export-import policy. Since the trade reforms in 1991, the trend shows that import of capital goods and project goods have increased. Increase in capital goods import is attributed by liberalised industrial policy which permits free import of capital goods at low import duty. Import of capital goods increased by 33 per cent in 1993-94 and 28 per cent in 1994-95 while import of project goods increased by 9.6 per cent and 43 per cent respectively. Among the import items in 1994-95, highest growth was in edible oils (43%) which resulted to overall growth of import of food products at 283 per cent. Despite favourable monsoon and rise in agricultural production and import substitution production measure why India fail to achieve trageted edibile oil production.

Net result of all external transaction indicate the foreign exchange reserves which in turn determines the balance of payment position. Improvement in India's balance of payment during 1992-93 and 1993-94 helped India build up foreign currency assets of RBI. Foreign currency assets increased from 6.4 billion dollars in 1992-93 to 15 billion dollars in 1993-94. Further rise in foreign currency reserves helped India to build up a total foreign currency asset of 19.6 billion dollars by the end of January 1995. This reserve is sufficient to cover our import requirement for nearly eight months. Large capital inflows from abroad and considerable decrease in current account gap are the factors that favoured India to increase the reserve. This has helped India to reduce its additional external debt burden. Increase in debt burden during 1993-94 has been only 740 million dollars. During 1994-95, the debt declined to 270 million dollars. The ratio of external debt to GDP thus declined from 41 per cent in 1991-92 to 40 per cent in 1992-93 and further down to 36 per cent in 1993-94. Consequent on all these favourable factors exchange value of rupee remained almost stable to dollars at Rs. 31.37 per U.S. dollar since July 1993 until 1994-95 end.

The question is whether relaking control and regulation on import and export procedure will create a trade surplus. Again, how long India can sustain a trade surplus. If sustained trade surplus appreciate the value of Indian rupee, what will happen in future. These are the vital questions that arise in India's export-import policy. Over the last three years India's foreign currency assets shows significant increase. For instance Foreign currency assets have increased from Rs. 14578 crore in 1991-92 to Rs. 47287 crore in 1993-94 and in 1994-95 it is estimated at Rs. 61651 crore. In a single year in 1991-92, foreign currency increased by 232 per cent. In 1993-94 increase had been 135 per cent. Strong balance of payment position and rise in foreign currency asset stabilised the exchange value of rupee first and then substantially appreciate the domestic currency. Continuous appreciation of exchange value will make export less profitable in the long run thus affecting export adversely. Such reverse trend has the possibility of ruining the balance of payment position because exporters get only fewer rupees for the dollar exporters. Therefore it is necessary to prevent rupees appreciation to such a degree as to make export business profitable. However, Indian situation has not emerged to such an extent.

13

EMERGING TRENDS IN INDIAN POLITICS

Gopal Singh, Rajinder Kaur*, Prem R. Bhardwaj**

Indian politics, like global politics, has witnessed dramatic changes during past one decade or so, particularly after the disintegration of Soviet Union and collapse of socialism as a model of economic development in East European countries as also in Yugoslavia. In this process of change, some new trends are everging in Indian politics and some dormant trends are being apprehended to influence the Indian polity by the academicians and it has become an important and vehement debate. This paper forms a part of this debate and is divided into five sections. Section one deals with politics of secessionism and violence in India and section two is exclusively devoted to socio-political consequences of so-called 'new economic policy' which has been formulated, obviously, under the dictates of IMF-WB and G-7. Part three deals with tension areas in centre-state relations which are leading to regional socio-political conflicts and upheavals. In section four, we have tried to investigate the process of institutional unbuilding and its implications. And, finally, fifth part deals with the question of leadership, national character and political corruption and their implications for Indian polity.

If one looks around and surveys as to what is happening all over India, one finds that the most conspicuous and self-perpetuat-

* Gopal Singh is Reader, Department of Political Science, Himachal Pradesh University, Shimla-5, Rajinder Kaur is Lecturer in Political Science, Correspondence Course, Punjabi University, Patiala and Prem R. Bhardwaj is Research Scholar, Department of Political Science, Himachal Pradesh University.

ing phenomenon is violence in one form or the other. "Peace" is rather an exception. The scope of this part of paper is limited to the discussion of secessionist violence, terrorism and state-terrorism on the one hand and caste-class, communal and electoral violence on the other. Any other type of political violence is beyond our purview. A brief perusal of the question of 'Human Rights' is interwoven in between.

So far as the politics of secessionism along with violence, terrorism and state-terrorism[1] attached with it is concerned, very surely, it is not a new phenomenon. We have seen all this in Tamil Nadu, Negaland, and other parts of North East India[2] in 1950's. However, the developments in 1980's and the first three years of 1990's in Punjab[3], Kashmir[4] and Assam[5], etc., have brought it to the forefront of national politics. As a matter of fact, secessionist violence in Kashmir has been internationalized[6]. Involvement of Pakistan in perpetuating terrorism in India by disseminating religous fundamentalism is the basic ascription to abet separatism and communal outlook. It is not simply the transfer of sophisticated weapons to militants which strangulates the egalitarian thought and perceptions but special teams of youth are trained to organise agitations, strikes, etc. and to tarnish democratic and secular image of India.[7]

Though historical, cultural, linguistic, geo-political and economic factors have played an important role in generating and sustaining militancy and terrorism, the predominant part has been played mostly by the ruling party at the Centre and partly also by other political parties including the regional ruling parties[8] in different states where secessionism has struck deep roots. For example, the people of Kashmir valley and the North-East feel not only economically deprived but also nourish a sense of discrimination in terms of their native cultures and local languages. The case of Punjab is a little bit different because Punjab is relatively more prosperous state. Here, it is the subjective perception of the Sikhs about the working of the Indian system which matters and therefore the formulation that "it is not only in economically backward areas but also in prosperous areas that secessionist movements may gain momentum at a particular point of time", seems to be true.[9] Even the most prosperous minority in a nation-state may demand secession. It is a sense of discrimination, partly genuine and partly perceived and imaginary which alienated a section of the Sikh youth from the so-called mainstream who took up arms for the creation of Khalistan in 1980's. In Kashmir valley once again, besides the role of Pakistan (ISI), it is petty-politicking by the ruling party at the Centre which has created a mess and tragedy we witness today.[10]

When the militants indulge in targeted and selective or indiscriminate and random killings, generally of the innocent people, the state reacts in its own way, with its own style, to counter the terror of the militants. The state through its various agencies, like the police, the paramilitary forces and the armed forces, and sometimes by also hiring groups of professional criminals, creates its own terror which has now become notorious as state-terrorism. The victims of this are also, by and large, the innocent people.[11] This ding-dong battle between the militants and the state continues with lot of bloodshed and up to a point of time when the people legitimize the otherwise illegitimate violent acts of the state. During this period, everything happens which not only harasses the people but also terrorises them through extortions, kidnappings, killings of innocent people by the police in fake-encounters and by the militants for their defined or undefined objectives, arrests without warrants and the use of third degree methods, etc.[12] That the root-cause of all this lies in the programmes and policies of the Central and state governments as also in the distribution of powers between the Centre and the states, is a point, which we will discuss a bit later on.

However, closely interwoven with the theme of secessionist politics is the question of ethnicity and nationality[13] which has become more important in the context of Indian situation after the collapse of socialist system and disintegration of erstwhile Soviet Union. Ethnic upsurges and ethnicity-based nationality conflicts have become the determining factors of politics in CIS (Commonwealth of Independent States). In India, the Kashmiris, the Sikhs, the Assamese, the Mizos, the Nagas, the Tripura tribals, etc., are demanding secession or/and right to self-determination on the basis of their claims of being a separate nationality and a distinct ethnic group. This is not to say that they did not articulate these demands earlier. The point we want to emphasise here is that have got a big boost after the disintegration of Soviet Union.

Another corollary of this, and in terms of distinct and separate identity of people of some areas, is their demand for separate States within the Union of India, for example demand for Bodoland (in

Assam), for Gorkhaland (in West Bengal), for Jharkhand (in Bihar, West Bengal, Orissa and MP), for Telangana (in Andhra Pradesh), for Ladakh and for Jammu (in Jammu and Kashmir), for Vidarbha (in Maharashtra), for Chhattisgarh (in MP), for Uttarakhand, Rohelkhand and Bundelkhand (in UP), etc.[14] However, so far as agitations are concerned, it is the demand for Jharkhand and recently for Uttarakhand which are important.

And before we take up other forms of violence, rocking the so-called Hindi heartland and other areas, it is relevant here to say a few words about the role of Human Rights Organisations regarding violation of civil liberties, democratic and human rights of the people in a situation of terrorism and state-terrorism.[15] It is correct that these organisations have to function under great stresses and strains. The Delhi-based PUDR (People's Union for Democratic Rights) and PUCL (People's Union for Civil Liberties) did an arduous but excellent job by investigating the acts of the guilty of the anti-Sikh riots in 1984 and prepared a 'Report'[16] in which the names of more than two dozen people including some top Congress leaders figured, though it is really an irony of the situation that none of them has been punished so far. PUDR and PUCL were dubbed as CIA agents by some Congress MPs in the Parliament. In different States of India, there are locally based human rights and civil liberties organisations which highlight acts of omission and commission of the governments concerned. Then there is Amnesty International which keeps a record of violations of Human Rights all over the world. The Government of India has recently appointed its own National Human Rights Commission (NHRC). And, above all, we have the Big-Boss, Bill Clinton, who feels concerned about the human rights' violations in Indian Punjab and Kashmir but never bothers about what is happening in the Pak-occupied Kashmir and Sindh and simply ignores the massive adid given to Kashmiri militants by Pakistan's ISI (Inter Services Intelligence) in fomenting insurgency in Indian Kashmir.[17] Moreover, for the last one year, he is keeping surprising silence about massacre of Muslims in Bosnia. In any case USA's own record about Human Rights, right from its intervention in Vietnam, Laos and Cambodia in 1955 till its latest proxy intervention in Somalia and through a superimposed war against people of Iraq, to say the least, is simply dismal and disgusting. And the US administration has no right to preach what it doesn't practise itself. So far as our local HROs are concerned, and in spite of the fact that they are doing an excellent job, as mentioned above, the problem with them is that they do only one part of the job and deliberately neglect the other. That is why, they are condemned by the government, as the front organisations of militants/nexalites, etc. The UN General Assembly Resolution on Declaration of Human Rights categorically states that the fundamental rights of every human being, of which right to life is the most important, shall be protected. The track-record of our local HROs so far has been that they have not cared for the killings of innocent people. Killing *per se* is bad but killing any one—a militant or an innocent person—without proper procedure and trial in a court of law, is worst. This simply brutalizes and dehumanises society and de-sentivises the individuals. This is exactly what is happening in India, particularly in peripheral and border areas. We must condemn both terrorism and state-terrorism.

Coming back to communal violence, and before we take stock of the present situation, it is essential to emphasize a few points. First of all, the communal rioting is as old as the pre-partition days and has claimed hundreds and thousands of lives since then.[18] Secondly, communal polarization in India today is much sharper than ever before. And thirdly, communal violence is potential and real threat to the unity and integrity of India, particularly after December 6, 1992, when the Babri Masjid was demolished by Hindu fanatics.[19] The demolition resulted in chain of communal carnage in different states leaving a big psychic divide between the two sister communities which have been living together for more than a thousand years. What happened on that day was not the demolition of a structure alone, it actually shook the very foundations of so-called secular and composite culture of the country. Not only the Muslims but also other minorities felt insecure. The bombing of Bombay, the business capital of India, was perhaps in retaliation to this humiliation heaped upon a helpless minority. The BJP-VHP-RSS combine probably harboured an ambition to rule the country through this act. However, the common Hindu masses, particularly the peasantry, felt disgusted and reacted against this type of fascist political behaviour of the so-called Sangh-Parivar. It has become evident from the recently held state-elections. It is not surprising, therefore, that the BJP lost six out of eight Vidhan Sabha seats in Ayodhya region itself. However, the damage has been done and it will take many years for the bleeding wounds to heal. The last point to be made in this context is that the so-called Hindi heartland as also Maharashtra were the worst affected areas of communal violence whereas the peripheral and border states remained comparatively free from communal carnage.

Coming to the question of caste-class contradictions in Indian society and the consequent violence, it is to be noted here that the caste hierarchy is an age-old phenomenon in Indian context because it dates back to Manu's time. However, it is only after the constitutional provision of reservation for SCs and STs introduced by Britishers and re-affirmed in 1950 in legislatures and jobs, and for some sections of OBCs since 1993 in Central jobs that caste conflicts have assumed new proportions. There was hardly any opposition to the reservations for the SCs and STs but there was vehement opposition to the shaby implementation of Mandal Commission recommendations by the V.P. Singh government, particularly in the North, when a large number of teenaged brilliant boys and girls immolated themselves, and consequently, the V.P.Singh government fell like a house of cards. However, the implementations of the same recommendations by P.V. Naras himha Rao's government on the basis of Supreme Court judgement by keeping the "creamy-layer" of the OBCs out for the purposes of reservations in Central jobs evoked little opposition from the high-castes.[20] In a capitalist society like India, poverty knows no caste or religion or region and all right thinking people earnestly believe in the upliftment of the economically backward sections of the whole society. However, we would like to emphasize here that even the reservations for SCs and STs resulted in the formation of elite-groups in these sections and it is these elite groups which have been pocketing the benefits of reservations of all types, thus leaving the vast masses in their own communities in a state of poverty and social and economic backwardness. The need is to demolish such elite-groups and to see that the benefits of reservations percolate to the poorest of the poor and by keeping the creamy-layer out. Some sort of reservation should be introduced for the poorest of the poor in the so-called forward or high castes to avoid any further confrontation.

Second crucial question is regarding the on-going debate about the caste-class convergence.[21] The crux of the debate is that the dominant castes constitute the dominant class also, particularly in rural areas. By the dominant castes is meant those castes which have ownership of land in the countryside. After the introduction of the reservations and also because of the upward mobility of the backward and the scheduled castes, this formulation is only partly true. What actually happens is that the upper peasant-castes do not hesitate even today to inflict physical injury including the killings and the humiliation on the scheduled castes in the rural areas. In such a situation, the poor among the upper peasent class join hands with the richer sections of that caste to teach a lesson to the scheduled castes. For example, this happened some-time ago in a village in district Allahabad when a scheduled caste woman was paraded naked in the streets of the village and the dispute was just over a piece of land between the son of that woman and the lumpen gangs of the dominant castes. So far no action has been taken against the guilty and a large number of scheduled caste families have already left the village. Ironically, this has happened in a state which is being ruled by OBC-SC combine i.e., Mulayam Singh Yadav of the SJP and Kanshi Ram of BSP. So, that is the situation on the ground even today, in spite of reservations and, above all, in spite of the OBC-SC government in the state. Therefore, the critical question to be pondered over and to be answered is as to who rules the rural areas?

Coming to purely class violence, it can only be said that a large number of Nexalite groups are operating in different parts of the country particularly in Bihar and Andhra Pradesh. The People's War Group (PWG) in Andhra is very active and has been able to mobilize a large section of tribal population in the state. During last few years, this group has become very powerful to the extent that they conveniently kidnap MLAs, Deputy Commissioners, high police officials and release them only when their arrested comrades are released. In the process of negotiations, again the catalytic role is played by the Andhra Pradesh Civil Liberties organization (APCL).[22] Prof. Hargopal of Central University of Hyderabad, along with Bal Gopal, the Prominent activists of APCL, generally perform the role of the mediator. So long as the exploitation of the tribals or for that matter of SCs and STs continues, such radical groups will continue to operate and in this process they have not only lost but are losing quite a few Naxalite activists in police-encounters, real or fake.

In the end, we would like to briefly refer to the electoral violence as also to the electoral malpractices. Barring the recently held elections in the six states, when electoral violence was at law key, but the malpractices were more or less the same as in earlier elections, there had been large-scale violence, booth capturing, rigging, etc., in the earlier elections and their possibility in future elections cannot be ruled out. Relatively peaceful and fair elections this time can be credited to the efforts of the CEC, T.N. Seshan, but T.N. Seshan as one individual cannot reform the whole system and T.N. Seshan is not going to continue as CEC for ever. Actually, what has happened is the lumpenization and criminalization of politics, use and misuse of government/official machinery, luring the voters through money and drinks, if possible, and through muscle power, if necessary. Lot many mafias and lobbies become active at the time of elections. For example, the sugar lobby; the liquor-lobby in almost all the states except the dry states and the forest mafias in the states which have large forest lands. Money is also pumped into the coffers of almost all the political parties by notorious smugglers, mafias and lobbies, stock market big bulls and some politicians do not hesitate to hire the services of decoits, professional killers and criminals and the wrestlers, who terrorise the weaker sections of the population either to vote for their candidate or not to vote at all. Secondly, almost all the political parties, including mainstream Communist Parties[23] exploit the phenomenon of caste and religion for electoral purposes. Since the elections are the very backbone of Indian democratic system, radical reforms are needed to stop malpractices and the use of physical violence, so that there can be free and fair elections and people can exercise their franchise to choose their representatives.

II

To illuminate the likely configurations of internal and external forces in national economy of India, responsible for the aggravation of present socio-economic crises, we have broadly divided our discussion under two sub-categories:

— First, representative policy perceptions of the Central planners leading to regional developmental imbalances, and

— Secondly, the more significant aspect of foreign involvement in the Indian decision-making process and its implications for Indian polity.

The concept of 'development', though a consequence of human inquisitiveness deeply rooted in human nature, yet is perhaps the latest, the most exciting and the most challenging study of human society in general and in the discipline of political economy in particular. It is rather a prolonged debate about the academic status of the concept, but one point is very clear that development in any form is the study of various determinants, their inter-relatedness and their implications for overall human advancement. The answer to the question whether development is exclusively an economic phenomenon, is certainly "no".[24] In fact, development implies a progressive change in human values touching every corner of national life. Our objective is not to explore the alternative measures of development at this stage. We intend to investigate different manifestations of unequal development at both the levels—within the nation-state and within the world community (which will be discussed lateron). Our objective is also not to delineate exclusively the neo-Marxist formulations which have related the concept of develolpment and its ramification as an unequal process, virtually with the structural need of bourgeois society in which the surplus from the peripheral regions is transferred to the Centre through various channels. However, here it is important to mention that developed countries have become the actual centre of inimical accumulation of capital from developing countries and as is clear from the very common fact that capital investment is proportionately related to capital return which confirms the argument that it is virtually impossible to reverse the flow of capital from developing countries to developed countries. What we want to infer from such statements is the fact that capital itself is responsible for uneven development of the society and furthermore, development is a very complex phenomenon necessarily having multi-dimensional facets with self-perpetuating sub-phenomena such as labour specialisation and differential value system.

By and large Indian economy is undergoing the process of reinvigoration, though languishly, at international level in general and at domestic level in particular. Before coming to the crux of argument, that is, the developmental imbalances, it is partinent to understand the real aspects of India's political economy:

— It is a vast country with substantial socio-economic heterogeneity.

— Taking into account the depth of socio-economic and political disparities it is very difficult to formulate universal development plan for the entire country.

— Instrumentation of objective policy in case of India is the manifestation beyond realisation.

— Finally, search for a capital is possible only by implementing the plans and also by upgrading the socio-economic infrastructure of the country.

From the point of view of semantics, one can understand, the ethos pervading the various complexities of Indian society. The issue at stake for all of us is not simply the smooth transition of economic substratum in accordance with the changes at global environment (which is being made more complex by supranational bodies) but an overhaul of socio-economic developments in post-independence era and a new pragmatic approach to surmount the challenges posed by new conditions. It is not merely a debate about imparting novel flexibility and dynamism to the recent economic reform programmes but also to acquire the adequate material basis which are urgently needed for the realisation of gainful political independence. The perplexing question emanating as a consequence of arbitrary behaviour of Central government with the states, emasculating the very basis of balance in national economic development and creating the precarious conditions for the survival of national life, is the intriguing perception of regional development by the Central decision-makers which in turn has not only marginalised the work-force but has also fed Indian economy with 'Euthanasia'. Can it be stated as connivance at the part of Centre which has held the banner of invigoration of Indian economy at the time of independence? The issue does not need an enunciation by simply a perception at least to understand the discriminatory colossus of Central authority while disbursing the 'grants in aid'[25] which the Centre has used in a sychophantic manner time and again. Its very purpose, i.e. to bridge the deficit of non-plan revenue budget of states, has become vitiated and its allocation has become the part of party politiking.

How far is the Centre responsible for the national uneven development? It is perhaps the most important question, answer of which is deeply implanted within the ethos and cultural values of political sorcerers at the Centre as well as in the states. As a matter of fact, fiscal imbalances cannot simply be interpreted in terms of monetary deregulation at the part of Union government. It is also on outcome of invariable revenue gaps shown in successive state budgets and it is an 'obligatory role'[26] of federal government to bridge the gap by the transfer of resources to the states, from where perhaps the intervention of Union government in state matters is inevitable. Problems do not arise from macro-economic setup all of a sudden.

The arbitrariness in priority determination, plan formulation and policy execution at micro-levels have made Indian economic setup cumbersome. Though, there is a sort of compensatory mechanism at the time of revenue loss due to over-centralisation of tax provision in one form or other, yet in normal process of monetary regulation, especially in the field of resource allocation, the states are indiscriminately maltreated time and again. Despite Finance Commission, an institution meant for supplementation of revenue to the state governments, the central authority has betrayed the states for the 'gap filling approach'. Whether Union government could define the 'single sensible criterion'[27] to disburse finances among the states, is always a burning question.

How far are Centre's fiscal devolution practices successful in enhancing the national development growth? To analyse such issues one has to be scrupulous about the nature of fiscal relations between the Centre and the states and also about the dynamic federal system amidst the widespread regional disparities. The routine patterns of Indian fiscal federalism manifest two broad objectives of our Union polity:

— On the one hand, the Central authority has to accept the responsibilities to bring up the backward states/regions to the level of developed states so as to accentuate over-all productive force of the country, and

— simultaneously on the other, it has to narrow down the progressive disparities among states and regions by bringing down the developmental gaps with the help of an objective and realistic set of policies.

Agony for India is the absence of a single formula for fiscal transaction between the Centre and the states on one hand and between Central or state authority and regions, on the other. As for example, special provisions for entire North-East, Tamil Nadu and Kerala highlight heterogeneity in the basic framework of the Constitution. Emergence of sense of exploitation among Jharkhand people is one of such remifications of Central or state authority's policy perceptions. Such single formula is, therefore, very difficult in case of India but the Central agencies, such as Planning Commission or Finance Commission, have to redefine the objectives of 'equalisation-cum-incentive'[28] in a more pragmatic way. The structuralist version of regional under-development can be traced in original form in the practices of Centre's attempts to conjure the particular region for one or other cause. The particular structural feature in terms of regional imbalances in India is the result of unrealistic approach adopted by the Centre. Is it merely an accusation of the two authorities—Union government at Central level and provincial governments at state level—against each other? How far does the Central authority get influenced by the justification presented by the states, does not need an elaboration. To make it more clear, we quote an incident when in 1967 Central government rejected the plea of Bihar state to declare it 'famine-stricken state'.[29] Therefore, post-1969 period financial relatioins between the Centre and the states or regions are being mainly influenced by partisan character of ruling political parties. Here it is relevant to mention that the Centre has hardly disagreed with the claims made by states but the question of assessment of claims and their reliabilities is also an important ingredient for maintenance of cordial relations between the Centre and the constituent units. Ironically, claims made by states or regions are never consistent with the assessment made by Central teaams of invesitigation which in many cases has led to delay for effective assistance. Obviously, such excercises give Central authority considerable discretion especially in the name of national integration.

The substantial discrimination in Central assistance to states is one part of the story. Another aspect, perhaps more important, is the process of priority determination and 'ad hocism' in resource allocation in various regions all over the country. The emergence of regional movements as strong defiance of Central policies and against the authoritative discrimination, is largely becoming the bane of Indian federalism and some of these movements are mostly the outcome of excessive financial dependence of states on the Centre. The role and behaviour of so-called autonomous bodies such as- inter-state council, zonal council, Planning Commission, NDC, etc., has been bitterly criticised by the advocates of state autonomy.

Now it is perhaps the right time to raise the question whether 'Structural Adjustment' dictated by the foreign agencies has fared well in third world countries in general and India in particular? The current resumption of multilateralism under the guise of capitalistic market system as the course of behaviour among nations is still overshadowed with the apprehensions of aberration. Undoubtedly, coming out of this obfuscated arrangement, the country may become orphan but forced imposition of SAP, DDT or GATT in Third World has inebariated the prospects of egalitarian society. Is the criticism of multilateralism a vacuous argument? According to us certainly not. Before coming to broader interpretation of various dimensions of foreign intervention in free and fair development of India and its socio-economic implications for Indian polity, we have to consider seriously certain assumptions, which are largely responsible for such development:

— Firstly, so-called multilateralism is vitiating the very basis of the sovereign status of weaker countries. Most succinctly, the major part of national sovereignty is being transferred either to supranational bodies or some other organisations.[30]

— Secondly, the diagnoses of SAP or DDT for sick economic setup of third world countries, are being authenticated by the Western countries which themselves are the cause of aggravation of these crises. It is not simply the question of doubts about authenticity of these measures which is arising in the minds of people of third world countries but ossification of perpetual dependent economy of weaker nations is perhaps the main apprehension.

— Finally, there are some valid reasons[31] to stigmatise the recent Western move after Soviet disintegration as a rhetoric strengthening of imperial structure in the name of multilateral trade agreements, globalisation and denationalisation.

India began with economic management in 1990-91 to place the economy on suitable path (at the moment when Soviet Union disintegrated and even after some basic structural changes). By enhancing the speed of 'commodity production'[32] new techno-economic paradigms have internationalised the production process which in fact deciphers the concept of competitiveness in the world market. The most interesting aspect of the analysis of reform programme in India from the Western countries, is its criticism for slower pace as compared to the changes taking place in the other parts of globe, especially in the field of production and transaction. The Eastern media have not only misinterpreted the ramification, but have also turned its face from the reality of crises agglomeration. Structural reforms as the condition for the assurance of so-called financial aid have jeopardised the primary human values without a considerable advantage. Restructuring was initiated ih the form of industrial policy reforms, public sector reforms, agricultural reforms, trade and exchange rate reforms and reforms in regulation Acts, e.g., MRTP and FERA. An appropriate generalisation of all these reforms lies in the simple argument that it is delimitation of state's sphere of activities in nation's economic progress. The statement does not need an explanation after realising the depth of Man Mohan Singh's deliberate submission to the IMF-WB conditions in 1991 to ensure the instalment of foreign aid from IFIs as a short-term solution for existing Balance of Payment crisis. The nature of conditionalities imposed by these institutions certainly did not provide the solution to existing problems, yet it gave a substantial period to Indian policy-makers to 'restructure' the entire national set-up on the principles of capital generation and capital accumulation leading the society to class profligacy. The discussion of success of these diagnoses as the measures to surmount the economic crises in developing countries, will manifest the large number of influential factors at this stage and as is stated about socialism that it has failed in its one form of practicability, similarly structural adjustment as an imported policy did not provide an amenable solution to the socio-economic problems of majority of countries especially Latin American.[33] But prospects of national progress at any stage of development is primarily controlled, regulated and accelerated by the functional reorganisation of state through its agencies. For this particular reason, we should understand the nature of crises in economic progress of developing countries aetiologically vis-a-vis nature of pact being imposed by foreign forces which can be significantly interpreted in the forms of four Ds—Devaluation, Denationalisation, Deregulation and Desubsidisatioin—which are being advocated as 'macro-economic stabilisatiion' by eastern evaluators.[34]

In the first week of July 1991 Indian government was pressurised to devalue the Rupee in two phases. Undoubtedly, government is responsible to make an appropriate adjustment of exchange rates in accordance with value appropriation of national currency. So far, as devaluation of Rupee was concerned, it is doubtful whether Rupee was overvalued[35] vis-a-vis major currencies. Though it could enhance the export profitability, yet prices of primary commodities would certainly go up especially for those products which are based on imported raw material. It is related to exchange rate mechanism and is a short-term measure and cannot provide a viable solution to existing financial problems. Is it a means specifically used to correct the 'fundamental disequilibrium' in commodity transaction and can't it help considerably in attaining the equilibrium in the field of exchange? Interestingly its weakness has been proved in many countries where the crises are taking more acute shape. Reason is quite obvious that subsidiary factors such as timings, occasion and existing exchange rate, influence the benefits of devaluation. By making the export cheaper and import costlier and with keeping demand as inelastic, the measure can never help in correcting the BOP deficit. As we know demand is relatively inelastic in international market as compared to decrease in prices of commodities (i.e., quantity/consumption at international market does not increase with the rate of decrease of prices) the devaluation under such circumstances can only worsen the trade terms in world market system.

The economic invigoration of a particular country can rightly be emphasised with the rate of increase in investment. But most important aspect in this direction is that not only in India but in almost entire developing economies, state revenue does not compose a substantial source of capital investment and, therefore, increased rate of investment in economy is only possible from big businesses, NRIs and MNCs. Will these sources up-grade the national economy in tune with speed of transformation at global level? Entire things lie in the nature of role played by state in directing the national economies on the right track. Free and frank invitation to MNCs and emasculation of mechanism of state control on the means of production may drag the state economic system to the evil consequences of capitalism.[36] Capital investment as a phenomenon has its own ingredients, such as basic economic infrastructure, market potential and maximum profitability. Do the factors such as unequal international division of labour, wide desparities in wages, labour costs between developed and developing countries and wide technological gap between developed and developing world, permit state to be withered away at once? This is what denationalisation means in which capital is supposed to play pre-dominant role in value determination of individual. The successes of privatisation and liberalisation which are being suppoed attainable through recomposition of the structures of commodities production and value allocation, depends upon the efficiency of micro-economic structures and as stated by Chossudovsky,[37] compressing necessary consumption leads to decomposition of national economy. Therefore, intensive denationalisation may destroy the indigenous basis of economic development of national economy.

Besides denationalisation, new economic policy is aimed at the enlargement of investment as a means to substantial development by encouraging the multinationals and NRIs through the reduction in the control of expansion and scrapping of protective veil on indigenous production units which may fairly be stated as 'deregulation' or 'decontrol'. Ramifications of such practices may be perceived in the form of delicensing the foreign investment which in turn would lead to derationalisation of capital investment, decodifying MRTP leading to concentration of capital in a few hands in the form of monopolies, and scrapping FERA which will open up the fields of primary commodities production to MNCs simply on the principle of maximum return. Such practices will have differential implications for different sections of people. Simultaneous increase in capital investment may provide partial relief, but it is doubtful whether this investment would decompose the reverse impacts of these policies such as unemployment, price rise, etc. Here we would like to emphasise categorically that the present concept of globalisation which cannot equalise the value distribution among the individuals and further course of relations might be guided by capital laws which would certainly be more severe for economically handicapped people in a particular nation and weaker nations in world community.

Another important measure being imposed by International Financial Institutions is desubsidisation of state services and also of agriculture sector which is perhaps the most important condition affecting value disposal system guaranteeing the socio-economic justice to the poor. In the broader sense of value allocation the desubsidisation would lead to collapse of institutions of civil society such as health, education, transportation, etc.[38] One can think of desubsidisation in market economy of the West, where for example per capita health expenditure is $ 1860 whereas in India it is just $ 21[39] and in developing countries desubsidisation would debar the majority of population from basic services. Though, subsidy expenditure in industrialised countries is greater, i.e., 18 per cent of GDP, than low income countries, i.e., just 6 per cent, yet its scrapping will severely affect India's consumer market which is vulnerable to bear the burden of primary services and also the cost of production of primary consumer goods, especially agro-products.

Besides these macro-economic reforms which are specifically short-term diagnoses to upgrade the weakening economies, the recent phenomenon which has cropped up along with the hilarity of globalisation, is multilateralism in the form of Marrakesh Treaty under General Agreement on Tariff and Trade. It is perhaps too early to predict the final shape of New International Economic Order. However, the validity of equal participation of national economies in world market system highlights the birth of multilateralism as a preconception of accentuated role of capital monopolies in industrialised nations.[40] Multilateralism in modern context is primarily an exploitative aspect after depolarisation and demilitarisation of International Relations. The very structure of multilateral institutions such as IMF-WB (IBRD), the out-products of Bretton Woods Conference is functionally controlled by a handful of countries and interestingly most of key decisions are made in private conclaves without public accountability by surpassing the democratic values of individuals.[41] Isn't it that centralisation of public decisions is phenomenally high in supranational institutions, higher even than those of communist centralism in erstwhile Soviet Union or Eastern Europe where perphaps the democratic values of individuals had minimum degree of integrity? Take it or leave it arrangement, the Dunkel Draft Text is certainly the vilification of democratic foundations all over the world. Whether it is annihilation or ossification of primary economic structure of developing economies, will become clear with the degree of change in human values after its imposition. The ramification of globalisation and liberalisation along with the GATT measures may be dismal for amenable economies like that of India where such measures are going to affect the maximum people as compared to any other country in the world, particularly in the form of marginalisation of work-force due to greater differential education of wages and labour. The capital monopolies will come up with new impetus not only in the field of production but also in the field of marketing and services.[42] What will be the accessibility of under developled economics in world market system if R and D will become an exclusive job of foreign capitalists[43] and, moreover, isn't it the externalisation of process of policy formulation for our own people having governed by so-called democratic government if our local skills and producing units are to be left emasculated in the hands of foreign capitalists or if wage-labour is being authenticated by a few handful multinationals? If we do not say it burglary simply because we are being left free to choose the participation in global market through this agreement, but for 'obvious causes'[44] we can decipher it at least an intriguing intention of minority over the majority of world population. Whether it is question of patent, or agriculture, or textile or that of services, we have some impeccable reminiscences which justify the argument that despite recalcitrance from contending party, i.e. the Third World, these would be used simply as measures to control the majority of world market for their petty gains. Option for India is not that whether we can discard GATT at first instance but certainly the degree of subjugation and flexibility of our national interest, which will perhaps guide the nature of relations in the era of unrestrained capitalism. To our minds, this perverted form of imperialism is the tree which was brought up under the auspices of capitalistic exploitation and unfortunately, today there is no force to oppose or at least to omit those provisions of agreement which are becoming the sanctions against the majority of developing countries such as issue of Intellectual Property Rights or of services. Peter Sutherland,[45] Director General of GATT, has apprehended that it is the beginning, not the end, of bitter trade disputes in the world, especially between US and Japan, US and China, US and Europe and between developed and developing world. He has further stated that now we have more than five billion people competing for the share of pie which makes conflicts all the more inevitable.

What are the likely implications of these covenants for Indian polity? It is question of tremendous importance in the contemporary phase. For assessing the possible impacts of on-going structural (mal) adjustment on Indian politics we have to assume that:

- There are some conceivable distinctions in socio-economic and political structure of India as compared to other developing countries (e.g. India's GDP is higher to many other developing countries, it possesses substantially better quality of economic infrastructure and it is having fairly consistent market),
- question of economic sovereignty is obviously related to political sovereignty of a particular nation-state,
- besides lower economic values, quality of life in India is being influenced by the social diversities which do not permit to impose some ready-made formula, and
- finally, it is today's reality that India cannot come out of multilateral arrangements for instance GATT or in brief it has to formulate some new model of development suitable to present conditions.

Therefore, possibility of foreign intervention in one or other form requires a deep Binsight and thought and also a pragmatic approach to find a nitch for India in the modern world. Though, hardly any reform imposed by foreign powers affecting the structural basis of agricultural sector has yet been introduced (for instance a specific amount has been allocated for agricultural subsidy in 1994-95 budget), yet structural adjustment in other subsidiary sectors such as privatisation of public sectors as a remedy for their sickness, deregualtion and denationalisation will seriously affect the investment and hence efficiency of agriculture sector where 70 per cent of Indian population is engaged. Reduction in public investment in agriculture and social services is likely to accentuate unemployment, poverty and gross marginalisation of overall productive forces and thus it will eventually lead to social conflicts.

India cannot be studied as a specimen in isolation of other sister countries of the Third World. Undoubtedly, the most important implication of today's multilateralism is externalisation of decision making process, but while contending a practical approach, any agreement at international plateform is based on give and take principle. The most important thing in this context is sustainability of bargaining power and an accurate judgement of national interests, because when we are talking about the compromise, one has to be very specific as to which interest we are going to compromise and what is the compensation for that. Whether there is subjugation of national sovereignty to supranational bodies or in front of Western pressures, we have to be clear and prudent about the obscured aspects within the agreement. No country can mortgage the fate of poor people and also the national sources flippantly. We have seen time and again when our Parliament (dominated by one party), a democratic institution, is perpetually becoming a puppet in the hands of foreign powers.[46] To our minds, human values in India are quite different as compared to those in Western countries and, therefore, our Parliament has to remain as our own istitution as it represents the 'will' of the Indian people.

New economic policies have raised another important issue of the (il-) ligitimate functioning of state institutions such as Finance Commission, Planning Commission, Finance Ministry etc. After imposition of economic reforms, it is apprehended that these institutions are losing functional status. Since these policies of restructuring and readjustment are being imported in readymade form and these policies are not being formulated in accordance to local needs and priorities but in close connection with IFIs. Capital import has become a prime objective and positive control of states on national economies is liquidating.

So far as the investment of foreign capital is concerned, it is again doubtful whether these dictates will really meet the needs of particular nation. Role of capital in equal development of a nation is challengeable on the basis of laws of capital accumulation and surplus transaction. Capital investment takes place on the principle of maximum return which is mainly dependable on economic infrastructure, such as transportation and communication, and availability of qualitised raw material. Rural areas in India lack a sustainable level of economic infrastructure which may remain untouched if state loses its hold in priority determination and, consequently, may create greater economic imbalance.

Moreover issues of Balance of Payments, Debt-Crisis, Debt Servicing, etc., are to remain within the purview of Indian economy for which no country or institution is going to help. All these conditions will perpetuate the drain of capital end resources from developing world to developed world. The nature of dependency and the debt trap will force developing countries to subjugate the greater part of their sovereignty to the so-called supranational bodies. Therefore, under these circumstances, India has to adopt some viable path in the face of globalisation and multilateralism.

III

Is it fair to characterise ever increasing tensions against the Indian Federal Authority in majority of states as unscrupulous defiance of national consciousness in broader sense? Attitude of the Central authority and leadership with regards to resource allocation, is perhaps the most important ingredient to convert Indian state into a 'Leviathan' in which constituting states are forced to proceed through self-perpetuating phenomena of secessionism, violence and insurrections, particularly, by the misuse of awarded or unawarded contitutional powers against the states. Whether it is the question of legislative powers of Centre (Art. 249) or the question of state emergency (Art. 356), Centre has always exhibited the power ruthlessly without caring for legitimacy or constitutional validity and Central authority does not need to issue the certificate of appropriation and the ball always remains in its court.

On the basis of unequal developments, over-centralisation of power in favour of Central authority, almost complete control on the financial resources and indiscriminate interference even in the state subjects, have collectively created apprehension about the smooth working of Indian federal system. It has been explained by Gopal Singh and Ramesh Chauhan,[47] that state politics does not operate in vacuum. Many factors play important role in shaping the politics at both the levels-centre and state. For instance ruling parties at the Centre and in the states have affected the course of un-avoidable interactions between Central and state authorities and also among the states. When the continuous interaction between the Centre and the States is indispensable, many problems in the working of smooth relationship between the two are obvious to arise. This is clear that the major cause for most of these problems is faulty policy perceptions of Central authority. Though, the conduct and policy formulation by state governments are also important factors, yet concentration of powers in the hands of Central govenment may fairly be identified as the most conspicuous factor which has vitiated the working of Indian federal system time and again. This process of power accumulation got quick fillip with the demise of value-based politics and statesmen spirit among the rulers at the Centre as well as in the states.

The most important implication of this power imbalance is berration from smooth working of federal setup and emergence of fissiparous tendencies which are, in turn, challenging the very basis of national integrity. The 'politics of violence', whether communal or caste based, or electoral, is widely becoming the characteristic of our national polity and aetiological study suggests that the base of such turbulance is deep rooted in 'politics of discrimination'—discrimination against the state agencies, discrimination based on ideological difference and discrimination simply on the basis of different ruling parties at the Centre and in the states. The most important manifestation of such political culture is accentuation of fundamental difference between the Centre and the states and sometimes even among the states.[48] The difference in policy perceptions of Central authority and state authority is clear from the fact that former had never paid any heed to develop the peripheral states or regions only for the fictitious reason that these are borderline areas. Now question arises can Central authority succeed in bringing these states at par with other states in nation-building process or more appropriately, in this nuclear age is any industry at Delhi or in other Central part of India safer than at Amritsar or Doda? Isn't that by ignoring the peripheral states or regions for one or other reason, the ties between Centre and states or regions have become more incorrigible? Such policies of Centre have affected the national integrity or for that matter national federal setup in twoways:

- On the one hand, as the consequence of such practices the regional imbalances have geared up the tension building process between Centre and states which is emerging as the chorus of defiance against the legictimacy of Central authority, particularly, after 1967; and
- simultaneously, on the other, the peripheral areas are being marginalized from the process of nation-building which, in fact, has propelled the secessionist movements. Manual power, especially the youth, of these regions is not assimilated in the national mainstream and, obviously, they are becoming an easy prey in the foreign hands.

In practice, supremacy of Centre over states has been established by several provisions[49] under Indian Constitution. Most important of these may be categorised as legislative supremacy (Arts. 249 and 254), Executive supremacy (Arts. 257 & 258), Financial supremacy (Arts. 270 and 271), Obligatory supremacy (Arts. 252 and 253) and emergengy provisions especially Art. 356, which have in fact obliterated the balancing machanism of Indian federalism by obfuscating its bases of co-operativeness and accommodativeness. Central authority has misappropriated these provisions by talking of threat to national integration. It has used these measures extensively and arbitratrily with the help of Central agencies which have reduced the sphere of state activities severely. Original philosophy of consensual and accommodative inter working of Centre and states has become inebriated with a twist towards the confrontational politics.

In original document of Indian Constitution, i.e., Draft Constitution, it is fortification of Central authority not only to play the supervisory role but also in order to maintain the unity and integrity of the nation. The voices for effective channelising of integrating forces had always ascertained from the Centre in form of statements such as that of States Reorganisation Commission[50] or memoranda of Central authority and there is hardly any evidence when Centre had seriously thought about the genesis and growth of sub-nationalism, regionalism or sub-regionalism. There were the states or regions particularly in 1960s which have expressed resentment against Central authority. According to our perception, attempts to suppress the regional or local apirations or forcible integration of local diversities (cultural, ethnic, tribal, religious, or caste based), no matter how pious is the cause, from the Central point of control or regulations, have in fact aggravated the problems and in some cases have aggravated the conflictual situations.[51] Therefore, it is evident from Kashmir problem, Punjab crisis, Jharkhand issue or for that matter from Bodoland issue that peace cannot be transplanted by Central authority, rather the solutions of local problems are to be arrived at by initiating the process of confidence building at the local levels.

A careful analysis of arising gap between theory and practices of federal spirit manifests in the violation of the principles of co-operation and accommodation. In fact misjudgement, misappropriation and maltreatment of local sentiments by the egoistic elites at both the levels, Centre and state, have vitiated the federal philosophy of Indian Constitution. Under the broad categorisation of issue between Centre and states, we can state causes for imbalances under three sub-categories:

— Primarily, the issues which have emerged as the consequence of irresponsible exhibition of constitutional powers by the Centre. It is superfluous to state that excessive suppression of sub-national consciousness in Punjab, Assam or in Jammu and kashmir has resulted in the demand for secession. Interference in the smooth running of local governments by Art. 356 or through the Central institutions like governor, has put question mark on the national integration itself.

— Secondly, marginalisation of regional identities from the national mainstream has by and large deciphered the Centre's intensions to interfere in the process of local developments. Suppression of regional movements in North-East, Uttranchal in Uttar Pradesh, Telengana in Andhra Pradesh, Jharkhand in middle-east India, etc., by the Centre, has further complicated these problems, and

— Finally, misappropriations of economic plans by Central planning bodies such as Planning Commission, Finance Commission,[52] etc., has been new set of problems in the form of regional imbalances. Though, even after the recommendation of special assistance to states under different situations by 'Central agencies'[53] it is still ambiguous whether Central authorities have worked desirably and it is pertinent to state that the emphasis of Indian Constitution on the Central dominance in the fiscal matters in Indian federalism has been ministerpreted by the successive governments in Delhi.

More interestingly, unnecessary involvement of Union government in state administration such as in the appointment or removal of Governor from the office at the will of the Centre, imposition of State emergency just for petty political gains and, moreover, the overruling of 'general will' by the 'Central will'—has witnessed successive political disasters. Most important of these is the unscrupulous use of Art. 356. Till 1967, because of political homogeneity, relations between the Centre and states were almost smooth. But thereafter, with the rise of opposition parties the nature of Central autocracy came to the top. Appointment of Ram Lal, an active Congressman, as the Governor of Andhra Pradesh, well against the wishes of NTR and thereafter his dismissal of an elected government from office in 1984, show the decimation of democratic spirit. Was there really the breakdown of the constitutional machinery in Kerala in 1959, in Haryana in 1967, in nine Congress ruled states in 1977 or in nine non-Congress ruled states in 1980? Floor-crossing drama was the most important cause of Central rule in Haryana against Rao Brindera Singh in 1967. At the time when situation was against the interest of Congress party, Governor called it as the failure of constitutional machinery but when it turned in favour of the interests of Congress party, he kept mum.[54] Though, it has become widely known that party in the power at Centre has successfully or unsuccessfully tried to topple the state governments ruled by opposition, yet as for instance most recently Goa Governor Bhanu Pratap Singh had dismissed D, Suza ministry just for nothing and had appointed Ravi Naik as Chief Minister arbitrarily. What could be the example of governor's irresponsible behaviour more than this? Ironically, Centre had always some conjuring explanation to justify its callous and maverick actions. Such actions have annihilated the very basis of constitutional spirit time and again. In order to save the democratic values and constitutional dignity Sarkaria Commission had recommended that Art. 356 should be used sparingly and the governor should be appointed in consultation with concerned Chief Minister.[55] But irony of Indian political culture is that the role of party politics in nation-building and upholding the democratic values, has become suspicious.

It is not only in the field of smooth running of state governments where Union authority interferes, rather it has been noticed at so many occasions when Central government did not assist state governments ruled by the opposition, in their development plans and, obviously, state governments lost their popularity among respective people and as a consequence fell a prey to the strategies of the party politics of Central government. Undoubtedly, constitutional provisions for fair allocatiion of resources are there but the nature of enforcing authority is always unknown or more appropriately, authority is tilted towards arbitrary Centralism. The argument proves its validity when one analyses the nature of relationship between Centre and states meticulously. For instance, in Himachal Pradesh Shanta Kumar's government was put under constant strains. This is evident from the fact that despite certain measures the state government could not come out of the financial crisis. But things reversed the course soon after the formation of Virbhadra's government in the state. From where the finance for developmental plans is coming this time? Undoubtedly, not from the state revenue but from Central government. This is not a single incident but it has become a part and parcel of policy of ruling party at the Centre. Therefore, it is rightly apprehended that while defining the degree of assistance from central government to state government, ideologies of political parties play a significant role.[56] Ideological differences on the crucial issues such as 'state autonomy', did not allow the state legislatures to unite and as a matter of fact, Central government used the state government run by same political parties as a strategic means to defeat the opposite political ideology at the national level. Our argument is that the Central assistance became the part and parcel of political battle-field in which states suffered and are, in fact, suffering heavy losses.

It is evident from practices of Indian federal structure that a number of Central agencies are involved in the aggravation of various tensions directly or indirectly. Besides the use of Finance Commission and Planning Commission, even so-called neutral agencies such as Election Commission[57] were not spared, to curtail the state autonomy, The role of Posts and Telegraphs, All India Radio, Doordarshan, etc., is important in nations-building but in India the behaviour of these agencies is full of ambiguities. To present the facts and figures of the particular issues as well against the realities, has become a ceremony for Central government. To prove any state government fallacious through the proveable or unproveable manifestations, is the emerging political mockery of Indian federalism. However here it is pertinent to state that in many cases behaviour of state government has proven fallacious beyond doubts. To be more particular, the repeated assurances were given by then Uttar Pradesh government headed by Kalyan Singh to Central government and also to judiciary to maintain law and order and to preserve the monument (Mosque) but Kalyan Singh broke all promises. It was an act of deceit not only with the people (electorate) but also with the democratic values. Refusal of state government to accept the Central paramilitary forces up to last moment, does highlight the irreverence of fundamental democratic values. This particular situation compels the scholars of Centre-state relations to think seriously about the perpetrators both at Centre and in state, and bring out the dormant and manifest factors affecting the nature of Indian federal structure. Ironically, Central government becomes active or remains passive as it suits its partisan purposes. Demolition of Mosque could have been averted if an appropriate action would have been taken by central government and national prestige could have been saved. Therefore, in brief the government agencies at Centre and in state have to work in close association and co-ordination for the success of federal setup. An accommodative approach is needed to prevent India from the course of another Soviet episode, where not only over-centralisation of planning and budgeting and party bureaucracy but also the maltreatment of regional, ethnic and national sentiments contributed a lot.

IV

The process of decline of various institutions[58] like Parliament, i.e., the Central legislature, executive, judiciary, political parties, bureaucracy, etc., started with the assumption of power by late Mrs. Indira Gandhi who became a symbol of centralisation as one person. First of all, she engineered the split of the Congress party in 1969. Afterwards, slowly but surely she went ahead with concentration of all possible powers in her own hands. She flagrantly violated the judgement of Allahabad High Court which unseated her as member of parliament and resorted to popular plitics by organising rallies in her favour and by hook or by crook retained her Prime Ministership but when the opposition launched agitations in Gujarat and Bihar under the leadership of J.P. Narayan, she clamped emergency and arrested all important opposition leaders including Narayan. There were two broad implications of this, one, it was beginning of the end of the value-based politics and secondly, it was the beginning of the decline of independence of judiciary. This also had an adverse impact on the functioning of bureaucracy as an institution and more particularly on the functioning of intelligence agencies especially, the RAW which was meant for collecting intelligence data from foreign countries was practically employed to keep a watch on the opposition leaders during the emergency.[59] All the civil liberities and democratic rights were suspended and terror was created in the northern states because of forced sterilisation in the name of family planning. People reacted against the atrocities committed during emergency and voted Janata Party to power in 1977 at the Centre. Janata Party did not behave in any better way and crumbled under its own weight in 1980 because it was a party comprising different ideological shades ranging from a rightist party like Jana Sangh and Leftists like socialist party with peasant oriented centrist party of Charan Singh. After assuming power in 1980, she again resorted to the old tactics of concentrating all powers and thus forcing the pace of decline of various political institutions. Rajiv Gandhi, her successor, starting with the image of 'Mr. Clean', ended up as a Prime Minister allegedly involved in Bofors, the shady deal. In 1989, again people lost their faith in Congress and V.P. Singh became Prime Minister with the support from outside of BJP and Communists. Rather than rejuvenating the declining political institutions, he came out with implementation of decade-old 'Mandal Commission recommendations'[60] for OBCs which saw a terrible agitation against these recommendations in northern states and V.P. Singh government fell like a house of cards. To counter the Mandal politics of V.P. Singh, BJP came out with its Mandir politics which ultimately resulted in the demolition of Babari Masjid on December 6, 1992 with lot of communal rioting and blood-shed.

To be brief, the pace of decline of political institutions has further accelerated in 1990s; and we have called this phenomenon as 'institutional unbuilding'. The most important implication of this institutional unbuilding is the weakening of legislature and domination of executive which in case of Centre means one man show, that is the Prime Minister, whosoever he or she may be. The second implication is that in spite of anti-defection law, smaller parties are split and one group is made to join the ruling party while it is in minority. This is how the minority Congress government at Centre has become a majority. Beside other things, this means that major objective of almost all political parties is to gain and retain power and not to bother at all for the value-based politics and this has resulted not only in degeneration of political leadership but also of legitimacy in public perception.

V

The paradox of transformation in the character of comprehensive and legitimate leadership itself reveals the contrasts and contradictions in entire Indian political system in a dramatic way. The unfolding differentiations in value distribution system and ever widening communication gap between the ruler and the ruled, have in fact undermined the viable conditions primarily needed for realisation of goals and objectives of democracy. In this connection, do elites of India, particularly leaders and politicians, realise the strength of vicissitudes in the material progress of human being that has been taking place vigorously all round the world at least for last one century? As a matter of fact, values of individuals, their enlightenment and liberation, their eventual co-operation for decision-making organism and, consequently, their streamlining in process of nation-building, make the national progress conceivable fact[61] and in its broader manifestation, this objective is defined in terms of cavalier involvement of every individual irrespective of her/his status and position in the state and society.

The present trends in Indian politics decipher almost a complete hiatus between the rulers and their responsibilities on the one hand and the nature of historical evaluation of national political culture on the other. With reference to modern polity, the concept of value politics has been overshadowed by the theatrical perceptions[62] of Indian conditions by its leaders and politicians particulary in post-Nehru era.[63] To muzzle the public opinion and, thereafter, to misinterpret the public issues, has become an unusual brilliance of Indian politicians. Can we expect the emancipation of the weaker with the help of institutions being controlled by politically philistine people? Can there be a free and fair genesis and growth of sanity and human values among the common men if our leadership is full of moral depravity. Any reform made to assure human values becomes ineffective because of degenerated politicians, especially at the grass-root level.

This is how today's leadership is different from that of Nehruvian era, which has witnessed a qualitative statesman-spirit deeply implanted into the personality and has also witnessed the symbolic optimism. After Nehruvian era, there has been a mushroom growth of pseudo-patriotic sentiments among Indian politicians. This is because, perhaps the basic intitutions of individual character building, despite the growth of political aptitude and stabler political opinion among the common men, such as family, school, etc., are perpetually losing the immediate, concrete and fundamental bases of truely patriotic personality development. The continuous decline in moral values of elites has raised the most important issue of role of 'political consciousness' in nation building, because the leadership as an institution is gradually working as a strangulator of human ecstasy, Is it not that despite poor political awareness of common men, leaders during Nehru era had some consistent values? Our argument is not the negation of universal fact that higher political awareness would certainly help in creating healthy political environment, however, it is more important to understand the various parameters of political awareness which obviously influence the genesis of egalitarian thoughts in human minds. Whatsoever were the causes for higher political morale among politicians during our early independent history but it is evident that the leadership as an institution at that time had acknowledged the responsibility to bring up the country from such a panic stage. The changes in Indian political culture have shown their manifestations in three ways:

— Firstly, corruption in every form, particularly political and bureaucratic corruption, is largely becoming a primary ingredient of Indian politics.[64]

— Secondly, there is specific degree of interrelatedness in decline of political morale at the level of national politics on the one hand and grass-root level on the other which, in fact, is deteriorating the strength of integrating forces.

— And finally, due to a perpetual decline in socio-political morality of ruling elites, particularly the politicians, there is dormant but potential common recalcitrance against the politicians as a class.

Most important implication of such political culture is loss of faith in the leaders and henceforth, the loss of legitimacy of the authority. To throttle the common values of the people, to abet election violence, to decimate the national consciousness and large number of such other factors emasculated the growth of strong nationalistic character right from the grass-root level. Notion of political consciousness, primarily related to strong and healthy national character, has itself become diabolic as it is being interpreted in terms of political heresy in favour of the minority (the rulers). Misinterpretation of local sentiments and local values by the politicians, has thrown India into a sort of political chaos. It is not only the managerial responsibility of politicians but they have to prove their accountability and legitimacy in the perceptions of common men. Today, it seems Indian politics has been assimilated in the politics of scams and scandles.[65] Is there any device to measure the valuable property possession of politicians? Can public accountability be used to check the growing political hoax? The answer to such question is full of ambiguities with the fact that political leadership in India is unable to rise above the temptation.

The perversion of our representatives in terms of criminalisation, corruption and communalism, it ascertains the growing apathy of public. Presently in India, political culture is being swept by indecisiveness of the leaders and moreover to retain the power by any means leadership may bypass the institutions[66] such as party principles or bureaucratic setup. The misappropriations and misinterpretations of important public issues have not only de-institutionalised the Indian setup but have also depoliticised the Indian state in the sense that the basis of political values is crumbling in the community of leaders. The growing lumpenisation of Indian politics may soon drag whole of India into the state of political chaos.

Finally, while concluding the entire debate, we categorically emphasise that growing irreverance and aberration of democratic values, political vulgarization, freak political corruption, inebriation of Indian political culture especially by lumpenization and criminalization of politics at grass-root level, and casteification and communal polarization of Indian society have, collectively, led Indian politics to degeneration. Besides, growing secessionism and fundamentalism in all forms within the state politics of India, the undue pressures from supranational bodies are likely to accentuate the process of unemployment as the consequence of marginalization of national workforce and perpetual price-rise, which will seriously and adversely affect Indian politics. What are likely configurations of these trends, is subject to some other subsidiary factors such as success of SAP, electoral reforms, etc., but continuity of these trends, as we see them today, would certainly lead to demise of democratic values and we shall not be far from authoritarian and fascist regime.

References

1. On violence, terrorism, and state terrorism, for different perspectives, see among others, Eugene V. Walter, *Terror and Resistance: A Study of Political Violence*, Oxford University Press, New York, 1969; Hannah Arendt, *On Violence*, Brace and World Inc., New york, 1970; Ted Robert Gurr, *Why Men Rebel?* Princeton University Press, Princeton, 1970; Douglas A. Hibbs Jr., *Mass Political Violence: A Cross National Casual Analysis*, Wiley Inter Science Publications, New York, 1973; Fred.R.Von Der Mehden, *Comparative Political Violence*, Prentice Hall Inc., New Jersey, 1973; Paul Wilkinson, *Political Terrorism*, McMillan Press Ltd., London, 1974; Gerald Priestland, *The Future of Violence*, Hamish, Hamilton Ltd., London, 1975; Richard Clutterbuck, *Living with Terrorism*, Faber and Faber Ltd., London, 1975; Edward Hyams, *Terrorist and Terrorism*, M. Dent and Sons Ltd., London, 1975; Paul Wilkinson *Terrorism and the Liberal State*, McMillan Press Ltd., 1977; Gopal Singh "Psychology of Violence," *Social Scientist*, No.41, July 1976; Sachidanand Pandey, *Naxal Violence: A Social Political Study*, Chanakya Publication, New Delhi, 1985; Stephen Seggaller, *Invisible Armies: Terrorism into the 1990s*, Michael Joseph, London, 1986; Lawrence Zelic Freedman and Yonah Alexander, (eds) *Perspectives on Terrorism*, Hindustan Publishing House Ltd., New Delhi, 1985; Randhir Singh. "Terrorism, State Terrorism and Democratic Rights,"*Mainstream*". Republic Day Special, Jan., 25, 1992, pp. 29-46; Ajit Singh Bains, "State Terrorism and Human Rights,"*Seminar, No.398, October 1992, etc.*
2. For details, see Phanjoubam Tarapot, *Insurgency Movement in North-Eastern India*, Vikas Publishing House, Pvt. Ltd., New Delhi, 1993.
3. Randhir Singh, "Marxists and Sikh Extremist Movement in Punjab," in Gopal Singh, (ed.), *Punjab; Past, Present and Future*, Ajanta Publications, New Delhi, 1994, pp. 369-377; Ajit Singh Bains, *op. cit.*, and Gopal Singh, *Politics of Sikh Homeland: 1940-1990* (forthcoming), Chapter 4, "Militancy, Terrorism and State Terrorism," Ajanta Publications, New Delhi, 1994.
4. For details, see P.S. Verma, *Jammu and Kashmir at the Political Cross-Roads*, Vikas Publishing House, Pvt. Ltd., New Delhi, 1994, pp.203-287.
5. For details, see, Myron Weiner, *Sons of the Soil: Migration and Ethnic Conflict in India*, Oxford University Press, Delhi, 1988 and Apurba Kumar Baruah, *Social Tensions in Assam: Middle Class Politics*, Purbanchal Prakashan, Guwahati, 1991.
6. P.S. Verma, *op. cit.*

7. For the details of Pakistan's attempt to inebriate the secular structure of India with the help of various organisations particularly ISI, see, Amir Tuteja, "Pakistan and Export of Terrorism," in three parts, *The Tribune*, Jan. 24,25 and 26, 1994.
8. Randhir Singh "Marxists and the Sikh Extremist Movement in Punjab, "*op. cit.*
9. K.R. Bombwall, "Ethno-Nationalism," *Seminar* No. 294, Feb., 1984, p. 52.
10. Randhir Singh, "Marxists and the Sikh Extemist Movement in Punjab," *op. cit.*
11. *Ibid.*
12. Ajit singh Bains, *op. cit.*
13. For details, see, Urmila Phadnis, *Ethnicity and Nation Building in South Asia*, Sage Publication, New Delhi, 1990.
14. For details on this theme, see Vinay Kumar Malhotra, "Separatism in State Politics, "*ISDA Journal* Vol. 3, No. 1, pp. 22-37.
15. Ajit Singh Bains, op. cit, Randhir Singh, "Terrorism, State Terrorism and Democratic Rights,"*op. cit;* and Gopal Singh "Militancy, Terrorism and State Terrorism,"op. cit.
16. *Who are the Guilty ?* PUDR and PUCL Report on anti-Sikh riots, Delhi, Nov. 1984.
17. For details of ISI and Pakistan role, see Amir Tuteja, "Pakistan and Export of Terrorism," and "ISI's Operations in India," *The Tribune*, Chandigarh, dated 24 January and 25 January, 1994.
18. For details see, Bipin Chandra, *Communalism in Modern India;* and Pramod Kumar, *Communalism and Communal Violence in India; An Analytical Approach*, Ajanta Publications, New Delhi, 1992.
19. On Ayodhya episode lot of literature, articles and books are available. See for details of controversy, Asgar Ali Engineer, (ed.), *Politics of Confrontation: Babari Masjid Ramjanambhumi Controversy Run-Riots*, Ajanta Publications, New Delhi, 1993, and Gyanendra Pandey, (ed.), *Hindus and Others*, London: Viking, 1993.
20. For two opposite viewpoints on the implementation of Mandal Commission Recommendations by V.P. Singh government and P.V. Narasimha Rao government, see K.C. Yadav and Rajbir Singh, *Unequal Citizens of India*, Manohar, New Delhi, 1994; and Gopal Singh and Hari Lal Sharma, *Politics of Reservations in India: Mandalization of Indian Society* (forthcoming) Deep & Deep Publications, New Delhi, 1994.
21. The debate started with the publication of Andre Beitelle's book, *Caste, Class and Power*, California University Press, 1965 and is still continuing.
22. For details of achievements of APCL in particular and other such organizations in general, see Randhir Singh's inaugural address to APCL meet, "Terrorism, State Terrorism and Democratic Rights," *op. cit.*
23. For the use/abuse/misuse of caste and religion by communist parties—CPI and CPM, see, K.Govindan Kutty, "From Class Theory to Caste Politics," *Indian Express*, Chandigarh, dated January 16, 1994, p. 7.
24. According to Michael P. Tondaro, development must encompass more than the material and financial side of people's life and it should be perceived

as multidimensional process involving the reorganisation and re-orientation of entire socio-economic interpretation of the concept of development has been redefined in terms of reduction of elimination of poverty, inequality and unemployment within the context of growing economy. For details see his *Economic Development in Third World*, Longman, Hyderabad, 1991.

25. It was not simply a recalcitrant complaint of the states against the Centre for distributing the 'grants-in-aid' among the states. For instance Haryana with the population of 1.40 crore was issued the drought relief of Rs. 16 crore whereas Nagaland with a population of merely 7.74 lakhs was given Rs. 30 crore in 1987-88. Defiance of state authority against the Centre's discrimination is witnessed by numerous incidents for example in 1988 Prime Minister released Rs. Three lakhs for Haryana to provide relief for flood victims which Haryana Government returned to Centre by saying that it is inadequate. For details see, J.R. Siwach, *Dynamics of Indian Government and Politics*, Sterling Publications, New Delhi, 1990, pp. 486-99 and also K.C. Markhandan, *Centre-State Relation: The Perspective*, ABS Publication, 1986, pp. 83-97.

26. Supreme Court has given the Verdict (coffee Vs. CTO) that revenue allocated to the union is not meant entirely for the purpose of union but has to be distributed among the states. Even those taxes and duties which constitute the Consolidated Fund of India may be used for the purpose of supplementary revenues of the states. For details see Durga Dass Basu, *Introduction to the Constitution of India*, Prince Hall, INC Delhi, 1992, p. 295.

27. Hemlata Rao has quoted K.V.S. Shastri while emphasising the distribution of tax-revenue among states on the principle of 'Single sensible criterion'. But feasibility of such criterion looks out of empirical approach because can there be any specific parameter to give a considerable thought to the needs of states? Moreover, single sensible criterion is perhaps more fictitious than empirical and as stated by Hemlata, may not be practical, rather may accentuate several problems. For details see her "Federal Fiscal Transfer: An Alternative Approach", *The Indian Economic Journal*, Vol. 41; No. 1, p. 108.

28. For details of the terms 'equalization' and 'incentive' see, Ibid., pp. 109-110.

29. After 1967, there is almost a perpetual phase of conflicts in Indian federation. In 1967, Samyukat Vidhayak Dal (SVD) governments, of Bihar made a plea for co-operation from Centre especially for the grain supply but the Centre rejected the request. However, lateron state government was allowed to manage from other states after relaxing the zonal food trade restriction. Similarly Central government had accepted to release the assistance to TN government of M. Karunanidhi in 1970s under the condition of supervisory role which TN government rejected. For details, see C.V. Raghavulu and B.P.C. Bose, "Centre-State Relations in Disaster: Mitigation and Preparedness", *The Indian Journal of Political Science*, Vol. 53, No. 3, July-September, 1992, pp. 314-31.

30. Etymologically, supranational bodies are those composed of independent nations exercising the rule of law based on equal respect for national sovereignty. In this particular sense the nature of GATT is ambiguous because to surrender the major part of national sovereignty, (i.e., decision-making), to it only for the cause of a few western nations, will strangulate the path of humane development in weaker nations. Does GATT theory

justify the replete regulation of trade laws of 117 countries, which are going to rectify the agreement? It is the strategy for weakening third world economy.

31. It has been proved time and again that so-called philanthropic attempts made to bring out the developing countries from the curses of economic crises, have become utter failure and almost every country has undergone the stifling of the economy after the adoption of these reforms. Patrick. Conway, the knight of structural adjustment, has confirmed the success of SAP in a very prolific way. For details see his "An Atheocratic Evaluation of Success in Structural Adjustment," *Economic Development and Cultural Change,* Vol. 42, No. 2, June 1994, pp. 267-92. But story of its success is quite different. No country in world could generate the capital as was propagated by developed countries. For details see, *Structural Adjustment Who Really Pays?* Public Interest Research Group, New Delhi, 1992. It is evident from the experience of Bangladesh that the package from outside cannot bring up the country from local crisis as IFI's stabilisation programme fed the national system with many problems such as—unemployment, perpetual GDP decline leading to reduction in saving and consequently, in investment, for details see, Rehman Shobhan,"Structural Maladjustment: Bangladesh Experience with Market Reforms," *Economic and Political Weekly,* Vol.28, No. 19, 8 May 1993, p. 27, also Gopal Singh and Prem R. Bhardwaj, (forthcoming) *Disintegration of Soviet Union and Changing Global Politics,* Deep & Deep Publication, New Delhi, 1994, Chapter VIII, and Deepak Nayyar, Indian Economy at the Crossroads: Illusion and Reality, *Economic and Political Weekly,* Vol. 28, No. 15 April 10, 1993, pp. 639-53.

32. Competitiveness of a particular country is controlled by its production efficiency, participation in world trade, quality of trade surplus and per capita income of that country. All of these factors provide collectively a sound base for the pronouncement of hypothesis that competitive advantage involves localised process defined by local culture, institutions and values. For details see Ramesh Diwan and Chandana Chakraborty, "Is India's Economy Competitive?" *Economic and Political Weekly,* Vol. 28, No. 45, November 6, 1993, pp. 2478-82.

33. The developing countries have simply turned up as specimen for western countries in which various trials are being applied to solve the local problems but in a conjuring manner, while sustaining the very basis of discrimination, i.e., higher stage of imperialism. For details of performance of SAP and its failure to solve the present crises see, *Structural Adjustment, op.cit.*

34. Entire reform package is being divided into two sub-categories—the stabilisaton Programmes at macro-economy level and structural reforms aimed at to change the very basis of the nature of relationship among the primary phenomena of production, capital and labour. For details see Michael Chossudovsky, "Global Poverty and New World Economic Order," *Economic and Political Weekly,* Vol. 26, pp. 2527-37 and also *Structural Adjustment, op. cit.*

35. Between 1980-1990, the Rupee was depreciated by 55 % against dollar, 50 per cent against pound, 60 % against Deutsche Mark and 72% against Yen that is at the average of 5.6 % per annum. Therefore, more specifically, devaluation is the relative depreciation of domestic currency in relation to some

dominating foreign currencies which is otherwise fixed in the process of exchange rate mechanism.

Devaluation of Rupee at a time when it is forecast that world trade and domestic economic growth would decelerate, such measures would not give expected results. It is widely accepted that deformation in macro-economic managment is responsible for devaluation of currency, yet as stated by N. Jabhar, the spculative transformation in domestic institutional setup is equally important. For details see his "Rupee Devaluation: Real Issue, "*Economic and Political Weekly* Vol. 26, No. 36, Sept. 7, 1991, pp. 2119-20, and Vol. 26, No. 29, July 20, 1991, p. 724 and also Jaya Mehta, "IMF and Indian Economy," *Mainstream*. Vol. 29, No. 40 July 27, 1991, pp. 7. 15.

36. Ironically, it is evident that 80-95 % of primary commodities production is being controlled by 3-6 big MNCs and these capitalists have their own priority options not only in the field of selective investment in developing economies but also in the selection of host countries. For details see, Arun Kumar, "Unemployment and the Structural Adjustment Policies: Worsening Crisis due to Loss of Sovereignty," *Janata* Vol. 47 No. 4, March 8, 1992, pp. 9-15.

37. Decomposition or recomposition of national economy is predicted on the nature of relations between compression of demand and supply. Reduction in cost of production would lead to reactivation of production to gear up the export or in accordance to external market. For details see, Michael Chossudovsky, "Global Poverty", *op. cit.*

38. Majority of Indian population household income (with 5 to 6 family members)is less than Rs. 1000 per month which means per capita income is less than Rs. 7. If subsidies are scrapped at once it will affect not only state services i.e health, education, transportation, etc., but also the public distribution system. Under these circumstances Michael Chossudovsky has stated IMF Package as 'economic genocide.' See his "India Under IMF Rule". *Economic and Political Weekly*, Vol. 28, No. 10, March 6, 1993, pp. 385-87.

39. For details see, Gopal Singh and Prem R. Bhardwaj, *op. cit.* and also Structural Adjustment, *op. cit.*

40. The term multilateralism is primarily related to nature of relationship between US on the one hand and outer world on the other. That means it was to be institutionalised to oversee the world trade. In 1930, US entered into bilateral agreements with 29 countries which highlights the fact that it has emerged with the transformations in capital monopolies. Right from 1947, Geneva Conference of GATT, US has tried to use the institution indiscriminately for its narrow economic gains. For details see, GATTASTROPHE, Public Interest Research Group, 1993, and also Kuldip Nayyar "Dunkel Requires Rethinking", *The Tribune*, March 30, 1994.

41. 'Multilateralism' and 'globalisation' have become a command action of a handful of nations and question is not simply that of the structure of commanding institutions but to determine who will be the major benefactor of interdependence. For details see Bernard Lown, "New World Order and Globalisation", *The Tribune*, Dec. 23, 1993.

42. The services such as education, health, transportation, shipping, insurance etc., have recently made a dramatic rise in share of GDP 70 per cent of the national income in US is constituted by the export of services and it is the

reason that US has successfully manoeuvred the world community to include services under the purview of GATT For details see, Gopal Singh and Prem R. Bhardwaj, *op. cit., GATTASTROPHE, op. cit.*, and also Surender J. Patel, "South and GATT Negotiations" Mainstream, Vol. 30, No. 10, Dec. 26, 1991, pp. 11-14

43. In this era of market competitiveness, can our national capital monopolies compete with foreign capital monopolies? Example in front of us is that of Pepsi Foods International which has almost bulldozed the Punjab Agro-Industries Corporation in order to become 100 per cent foreign company. Both Voltas, a Tata company, and Punjab Agro-Industries, are being forced to bear heavy losses for years. For details see *The Tribune*, 4th April, 1994. p. 1. Besides the above ramification, the recent GATT agreement would effect research and development India's state monopolies do not have sufficient funds to conduct fundamental research, especially in the field of pharmaceutical research and it is doubtful whether MNCs would invest on research and development in accordance with local needs and priorities. Same would be the case with agriculture. It is aberration of state acts that nation should up-grade and protect the growing national monopolies which would put a substantial check on growth and consolidation of foreign monopolies (S.K.Goyal, "MNCs and Self Reliance" a paper presented to Public Policy and Planning Division IIPA, New Delhi), as native capitalists are economically so weak that even state itself would become helpless to maintain their entities. For details of various dimensions of recent GATT assignments see Nilima Chandiramani, GATT and India", *Mainstream* Vol. 32, No. 22, April 26, 1994, pp. 7-10 and 30-35.

44. For example, US based Intellectual Property Coalition, a grouping of 13 major companies, pressurised their government to press for intellectual property protection to be brought under GATT rules, with threat of trade sanctions, changes in investment measures and patents/IPRs/regime. For details see *GATTASTROPHE, op. cit.*

45. *Financial Express*, April 17, 1994, p.1.

46. For instance, Finance Minister, Man Mohan Singh's prior communication with IFIs about the preparation of pre-budget document in 1991-92 generate such apprehensions in the minds of people.

47. Apathy of Central government even to consider the genuine demands of state governments or the regions, especially that of autonomy in allocation of resources, has resulted in many unforeseen developments in majority of the states. Punjab crisis, Assam Crisis, Bodoland issue, of Jharkhand, etc., are the examples of the policy discrimination by the Cental authority which did not help to generate local skill and local revenue of the regions. For details of excesses of Central government on the state goverments, see Gopal Singh and Ramesh Chauhan, "Dynamics of state Politics in India", *ISDA Journal*, Vol. 3, No. 1, Jan-March 1993, pp. 15-21.

48. Recent recalcitance shown by Rajasthan government along with some other states, to implement some of the GATT provisions authenticates the statement. Rajasthan government and three other states have already moved to the Supreme Court against Art. 253 of Indian Constitution whereas other states ruled by Congress (I) have given their consent to the Text.

49. For detailed analysis of these provisions, see Durge Das Basu, *Introduction to the Constitution of India, op. cit*, pp. 287-328.

50. For details see *States Reorganisation Commission Reports"*.
51. In fact, it is not only the exercise of statutory provisions by Central authority rather the ways in which it has tried to solve the local issues. As stated in *Document on Centre-State Relations* by West Bengal government, published in *Journal of Constitutional and Parliamentary Studies,* the democratic aspiration of common people cannot be authenticated from the centre rather the cultural, ethnic, subnational or regional identities are to be respected. Centre has to work as an integrating force between various diversities and its subversive or suppressive activities will lead to the balkaoisation or fissiparous tendencies. For details see also Sandeep Shastri, "Indian Federalism and National Integration-A Critique," *The Indian Journal of Political Science,* Vol. 51, No. 2, April-June 1990, pp. 172-185.
52. Planning Commission is extra constitutional body and deals with plan expenditure and plan priorities whereas Finance Commission is a constitutional body which primarily deals with the Central assistance to the states.
53. For details of priorities evaluation and Value allocation in financial matters, see different *Reports of Finance Commission,* Government of India Publication. Fourth Finance Commission in 1965 had advised the Union Government to adopt flexible approach while allocating the resources to the states which are facing natural calamities.
54. Role of Governor in accordance with constitution is a myth or more appropriately, right from his appointment Governor is made as an instrument of party politics and behaves paradoxically under the regular dictates of central rule without caring for democratic values of individuals. Moreover petty politicking has become the culture of India's federal setup in such a way that, for instance, Rao Birendra Singh's ministry was dismissed simply on the grounds of defection in 1967 but on the same day with the help of defectors, ministry of P.C. Gosh was installed in West Bengal. For details see, J.R. Siwach, *op. cit,* pp. 521-36.
55. For details see *Reports of the Commission on Centre-State Relations,* New Delhi, 1988.
56. It has been emphasised in second volume of Sarkaria Commission report that the differences in ideologies and attitudes and thereafter some differential and biased treatments have been the outcome of centre's policy perceptions vis-a-vis state. For details of ideological apprehensions in guiding the centre-state relations, see *Report of Commission on Centre-State Relations,* Vol. 2, Government of India Publication, New Delhi, 1988. The divergence in ideological principles has not only created a cleavage between Centre and States but have compelled the states to debar from mutual assistance on common issues. Approach of Manipur and Rajasthan governments for strengthening the central powers and demand of 'state autonomy' expressed by Rajamanna Committee in TN in early seventies and repeated appeals of Communist Party of India to uphold the dignity of state governments, are some of the major developments where the political ideologies have perpetuated the confrontation. For broader analysis of Reports of Sarkaria Commission see S. Saraswathi, "Prescriptive Centralisation: Sarkaria Commission's Prescription for Union-State Relations in India". *Indian Journal of Political Science,* Vol. 50, No. 2, April-June 1989, pp. 191-208.

57. Election Commission before the installation of Rao Government in Delhi and after the declaration of majority of election results, postponed the Punjab elections just before hours which clarifies the arguments that the role and functions of union agencies are controlled and guided by central government directly or indirectly and are used as a tactic for political dominance.
58. Widespread fear of political instability particularly in early 1990s, criminalisation of politics and politics of revivalism and subnationlism, have collectively brought the functioning of the state institutions under grave contradictions. Undoubtedly, paradox of Indian polity is widespread socio-economic diversities but state has to prove its accountability, through its institutions, to the people. For details of institutional unbuilding in India, see, Llyod I. Rudolph and Susaune Hoeber Rudolph, *In Pursuit of Lakshmi*, Orient Longman, Chicago, 1987.
59. For details of excesses committed by Indian goverent during emergency period and consequently, the perpetual demise of political institutions, see Myron Weiner, *The Indian Paradox: Essays in Indian Politics*, Sage Publication, New Delhi, 1989.
60. For details of socio-economic and political implications of the implementation of Mandal Commission by V.P. Singh government see, Gopal Singh and Hari Lal Sharma, *Politics of Reservation: Mandalisation of Indian Society*, (forthcoming) Deep and Deep Publications, New Delhi, 1994.
61. Here most important thing to note is the strength and quality of native consciousness such as ethnic, caste and class consciousness, and its relationship with the process of national development and is likely to mitigate state institutions meant for even national progress. For details of genesis of minority consciousness and its implications on Indian polity see, Myron Veiner, *The Indian Paradox: Essays in Indian Politics*, *op. cit.*
62. The role of politicians in perpetuating the socio-political chaos cannot be overlooked by calling it simply as connivance but there are lots of evidences when popular leaders have behaved conjuringly and blasphemy has become a popular practice of Indian politics. An optimistic political dissent is undoubtedly a healthy process for democracy but misinterpretation of crucial issues maul the national prestige. Defeat of Congress party in 1977 and 1989 may fairly be interpreted as the consequence of imposition of Congress culture over the national polity. For details of deculturisation of national polity see, Lloyd I. Rudolph and Susaune Hoeber Rudolph. *op. cit.* and Myrin Weiner, *The Indian Paradox*, *op. cit.*
63. In Indian political history, Nehru era is stated as chrismatic era of Indian leadership. Leaders had not only high sense of public accountability but had also the chrismatic outlook which got maligned with the advent of Indira Gandhi on the national political map. For detail see, Rudolph and Rudolph, *op. cit.*, and also Myron Weiner, *The Indian Paradox*, *op. cit.*
64. There has been a continuous decline in the moral character of elites who are grabbing the advantages of surplus at the cost of primary needs of the poor and consequently, agglomerating the socio-political problems. For instance, a powerful nexus of bureaucrats, politicians and contractors is siphoning off the money for decades in J & K. Callousness of State administrative machinery vis-a-vis local people has been of unprecedented scale. Can there

be any other example of depravity of leadership when local leaders with administrators and local contractors have drawn a sum of Rs. 22 lakhs for constructing Dharati-Panjani road in Balakote block which was built by army? Same is the case with Sajota Road. What can poor illiterate inhabitants of this border areas do against their own leaders who have thrown them to the state of dilapidation? Such incidents are obvious to challenge the public accountability of politicians who have adopted the politics as a career on business line not with the intentions of social services. For details of the ever demnable nexus of elites in Poonch and Rajouri destricts of J & K see, S.M.A. Kazmi, "Graft Bordering on Loot in Poonch and Rajouri", *Indian Express*, March 4, 1994, p. 1.

65. Was latest security scam simply a financial deregulation in connivance with national leaders? The involvement of our top national leaders in this scam cannot be ruled out in single voice. Most interesting thing about such corruption is that Rajiv's government was thrown out of office for the Bofors scandle of Rs. 64 crore but Narasimha Rao government is quite comfortable even after the mega-scam? Similarly role of big business in India is having substantial change with the fact that the IFIs are assuming their role.

66. The malaise of moral depravity among politicians is heading our constitutional institutions to virtual collapse. Indian democracy is losing its representative character and depoliticisation of Indian polity is being widely assimilated as political culture. For details see, Rajni Kothari, "Area of Darkness", Seminar, 399, November, 1992, pp. 14-17.

Index